The Midwest

Titles in the series:

The Northeast
The Southeast
The Midwest
The West
The Southwest

The
Midwest

GREENWOOD PRESS
Westport, Connecticut • London

Library of Congress Cataloging-in-Publication Data

Creative Media Applications
  How geography affects the United States/Creative Media Applications.
  p. cm.
  Summary: Explores the ways in which geography has affected the lives of the people of the United States.
  Includes bibliographical references (p.).
  Contents: v.1. Northeast — v.2. Southeast — v.3. Midwest — v.4. West — v.5. Southwest.
  ISBN 0-313-32250-3 (set) — 0-313-32251-1 (Northeast) — 0-313-32252-X (Southeast) — 0-313-32253-8 (Midwest) — 0-313-32254-6 (West) — 0-313-32255-4 (Southwest)
  1. United States — Geography — Juvenile literature. 2. Human geography — United States — Juvenile literature. 3. United States — History, Local — Juvenile literature. 4. Regionalism — United States — Juvenile literature. [1. United States — Geography.] I. Creative Media Applications.

E161.3.H69 2002
304.2'0973—dc21   2002075304

British Library Cataloguing in Publication Data is available.

Library of Congress Catalog Card Number: 2002075304
ISBN: 0-313-32250-3   (set)
           0-313-32251-1   (Northeast)
           0-313-32252-X   (Southeast)
           0-313-32253-8   (Midwest)
           0-313-32254-6   (West)
           0-313-32255-4   (Southwest)

First published in 2002

Greenwood Press, 88 Post Road West, Westport, CT 06881
An imprint of Greenwood Publishing Group, Inc.
www.greenwood.com

Printed in the United States of America

The paper used in this book complies with the Permanent Paper Standard issued by the National Information Standards Organization (Z39.48–1984).

10   9   8   7   6   5   4   3   2   1

A Creative Media Applications, Inc. Production
Writer: Robin Doak
Design and Production: Fabia Wargin Design, Inc.
Editor: Matt Levine
Copyeditor: Laurie Lieb
Proofreader: Tania Bissell
AP Photo Researcher: Yvette Reyes
Consultant: Dean M. Hanink, Department of Geography,
    University of Connecticut
Maps: Ortelius Design

Photo Credits:
Cover: ©Photodisc, Inc.
AP/Wide World Photographs *pages:* ix, 6, 10, 11, 19, 20, 23, 24, 27, 29, 41, 43, 44, 46, 52, 57, 59, 61, 67, 70, 74, 77, 79, 84, 88, 89, 91, 93, 94, 101, 107, 108, 110, 115, 120, 123, 124
©Photodisc, Inc. *pages:* viii, 3, 5, 118
©CORBIS *pages:* 8, 18, 35, 77, 103, 105
©Bettmann/CORBIS *pages:* 54, 69, 72, 106
©Layne Kennedy/CORBIS *page:* 38
©Tom Bean/CORBIS *page:* 40
©Richard Hamilton Smith/CORBIS *page:* 117

Contents

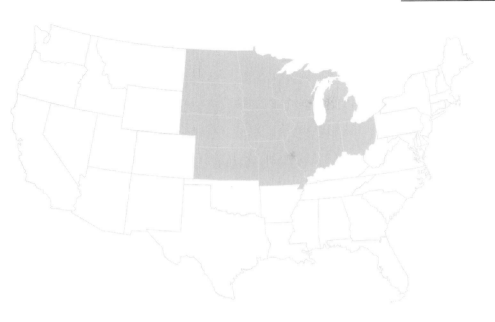

Introduction

The Midwest region of the United States is bordered by the Northeast and Southeast regions to the east, the Southeast and Southwest regions to the south, the West region to the west, and Canada to the north. There are twelve states in the Midwest: Illinois (il-ih-NOY), Indiana, Iowa, Kansas, Michigan (MISH-ih-gan), Minnesota, Missouri, Nebraska, North Dakota, Ohio, South Dakota, and Wisconsin.

The Midwest has a varied landscape, from the rolling plains and prairies to the rugged peaks and hills of the Ozarks and Black Hills. Some of the most important waterways of the nation are located in the Midwest, including the Mississippi and Missouri Rivers and the Great Lakes. These waterways played a key role in the exploration, settlement, and economic development of the United States.

The climate of the Midwest is also varied. Toward the northernmost part of the region, temperature extremes are common—freezing temperatures in the winter, hot weather in the summer.

The Nation's Breadbasket

Before European and American explorers began venturing into the Midwest, many Native American tribes lived in the region. Prominent tribes in the Midwest included the Sioux (SOO), Pawnee, and Cheyenne (shye-ANN) on the plains; the Ojibwa (oh-JIB-wah) and Iroquois (IHR-uh-kwoy) near the Great Lakes; and the Osage in the Ozarks. On the plains, native peoples depended upon the huge herds of bison, or buffalo, for food, clothing, and shelter.

Huge herds of bison once roamed the Great Plains.

Many of the earliest explorers in the region were French trappers and traders. As a result, some of the first settlements in the Midwest were founded as French trading posts. In 1803, the United States purchased all the land west of the Mississippi River from France. The Louisiana Purchase doubled the size of the United States and opened up the Midwest to settlement. Soon, pioneers from the Northeast and Southeast were heading into the region, hoping to find land and prosperity there.

By 1900, thousands of families had moved west to work the prairies and plains. They found that the Midwest was the perfect place to feed a growing nation. Farmers cultivated the fertile soil, growing wheat, corn, soybeans, and other crops. The area soon became known as the Breadbasket of the Nation.

The area is rich in natural resources, including iron, lead, coal, oil, and granite. Today, the Midwest is also known as an important industrial area. Steel, cars, rubber, electronics, ships, and aircraft are all produced in the region. Cleveland, Ohio; Chicago, Illinois; Detroit, Michigan; Milwaukee, Wisconsin; and St. Louis, Missouri are all major manufacturing centers of the Midwest.

Downtown Chicago, Illinois is famous for its tall buildings. The first modern skyscraper was built in Chicago in 1885.

STATE BIRTHDAYS

After the Louisiana Purchase in 1803, settlement west of the Mississippi picked up.

State	Capital	First Permanent Settlement	Date of Statehood	Order of Statehood
Illinois	Springfield	Cahokia, 1699	Dec. 3, 1818	21
Indiana	Indianapolis	Vincennes, 1732	Dec. 11, 1816	19
Iowa	Des Moines	Dubuque, 1833	Dec. 28, 1846	29
Kansas	Topeka	Fort Leavenworth, 1827	Jan. 29, 1861	34
Michigan	Lansing	Sault Ste. Marie, 1668	Jan. 26, 1837	26
Minnesota	St. Paul	Fort Snelling, 1819	May 11, 1858	32
Missouri	Jefferson City	Ste. Genevieve	Aug. 10, 1821	24
Nebraska	Lincoln	Bellevue, 1823	Mar. 1, 1867	37
North Dakota	Bismarck	Pembina, 1812	Nov. 2, 1889	39
Ohio	Columbus	Marietta, 1788	Mar. 1, 1803	17
South Dakota	Pierre	Fort Pierre, 1817	Nov. 2, 1889	40
Wisconsin	Madison	Green Bay, 1701	May 29, 1848	30

MORE STATE STATS

The largest state in the Midwest is Kansas, with nearly 82,000 square miles (213,200 square kilometers) of land. The smallest is Indiana. Here, the Midwest states are ordered from smallest to largest.

State	Size (land and water)	Size Rank	Population	State Rank
Indiana	35,870 square miles (93,262 square kilometers)	38	6,080,485	14
Ohio	40,953 square miles (106,478 square kilometers)	35	11,353,140	7
Wisconsin	54,314 square miles (141,216 square kilometers)	25	5,363,675	18
Iowa	56,275 square miles (145,752 square kilometers)	23	2,926,324	30
Illinois	56,400 square miles (146,076 square kilometers)	24	12,419,293	5
Michigan	56,809 square miles (147,703 square kilometers)	22	9,938,444	8
Missouri	68,819 square miles (178,929 square kilometers)	21	5,595,211	17
North Dakota	68,994 square miles (179,384 square kilometers)	17	642,200	47
South Dakota	75,898 square miles (197,335 square kilometers)	16	754,844	46
Nebraska	76,878 square miles (199,882 square kilometers)	15	1,711,263	38
Minnesota	79,617 square miles (207,004 square kilometers)	14	4,919,479	21
Kansas	82,282 square miles (213,933 square kilometers)	13	2,688,418	32

NOTE: All metric conversions in this book are approximate.

Black Hills

1

opposite:
Conestoga
wagons similar to
those used by the
pioneers who
moved west,
stand in front of
Eagle Rock near
Scotts Bluff,
Nebraska.

The Black Hills are a mountain range in South Dakota and Wyoming. Covering about 6,000 square miles (15,600 square kilometers), the hills are an area of high peaks, deep canyons, subterranean (sub-terr-AY-nee-an) caves, and unusual rock formations. Once three times their current size, the mountains have been worn down by wind and water erosion since they were first formed millions of years ago.

At 7,242 feet (2,173 meters), Harney Peak is the highest mountain in the range and in the state of South Dakota. Other towering peaks in the Black Hills include Terry Peak, Custer Peak, Ragged Top Mountain, and Crow Peak. Fascinating rock formations in the hills include Devil's Tower, a 1,280-foot (384-meter) volcanic formation, as well as Bear Butte (BYOOT), a tall buttress of lava and rock.

WHAT'S IN A NAME?

The Sioux (SOO) people called the peaks *paha sapa,* meaning "the hills that are dark." They gave the mountains their name because of the dark pine forests covering the peaks.

Settlement

The first humans to settle near the Black Hills were Native American tribes. These tribes included the Kiowa (KYE-oh-wuh), Cheyenne (shye-ANN), Pawnee, and Crow people. After the 1700s, the strongest group in the region was the Sioux (SOO). Many native groups considered the hills sacred places. They often went into the mountains for religious (ree-LIH-jus) ceremonies (SEHR-uh-moh-neez). Some of these rites lasted several days.

The first Europeans to visit the area were François (fran-SWAH) and Louis-Joseph de la Vérendrye (vayr-ahn-DREE) in 1743. These French brothers were trappers and traders in search of beaver pelts and other animal skins. In 1804, the Lewis and Clark expedition passed by the area on its way to the Pacific (puh-SIFF-ik) coast.

The first nonnatives to cross the mountains were led by Jedediah Strong Smith in 1823. The crossing was difficult: Smith's party was abandoned by their guide and attacked by grizzly bears. Smith himself received a scar from one big bear that he would carry for the rest of his life. Another famous Black Hills mountain man was Hugh Glass. Attacked by a grizzly and left for dead by his companions, he managed to crawl more than 200 miles (320 kilometers) in seven weeks to get to the nearest fort for help.

Because of the rugged terrain, deadly animals, and hostile native tribes, American settlers mostly considered the Black Hills an undesirable area. In 1868, the Black Hills were set aside "forever" for the Sioux people under the Treaty of Laramie. The hills, plus all of the southern Dakota Territory west of the Missouri, became known as the Great Sioux Reservation.

Gold in the Hills

During the mid-1800s, many people believed that the Black Hills were filled with gold. Once the region was given to the Sioux, however, gold prospecting was forbidden. In 1874, Lieutenant Colonel George Armstrong Custer led a military expedition into the hills. Part of Custer's group included miners and geologists. The miners soon found gold, sparking a huge rush of people to the area hoping to strike it rich.

At first, the U.S. government tried to honor its treaty with the Sioux and keep gold prospectors away. Many miners crept into the Black Hills anyway, risking attacks by angry Sioux. Other people began to demand that the government allow miners into the area. Bowing to pressure, the U.S. government tried to buy mineral rights to the Black Hills. When the Sioux refused to sell, the military was pulled out of the area. With no one to stop them, thousands of miners poured into the mountains, looking for gold.

The Mount Rushmore National Memorial rises out of the Black Hills of South Dakota. The likenesses of four American presidents are carved into the face of the mountain.

This early twentieth-century photograph shows "The Wild Bunch." From left to right are Henry Longabaugh, (the Sundance Kid), William Carver, Ben Kilpatrick (the Tall Texan), Harvey Logan (Kid Curry), and Robert LeRoy Parker (Butch Cassidy).

Towns sprang up around the mining areas in the Black Hills. Many of the towns started out as nothing more than a group of tents. However, as more people made their way into the area, the towns prospered and grew to include stores, hotels, laundries, saloons, and gambling parlors.

The towns were often lawless, wild, and dangerous. Infamous outlaws who got their start in the Black Hills area include Henry A. Longabaugh, also known as the Sundance Kid; Frank James, brother of Jesse; and William Chambers, known as Persimmon Bill, a famous stagecoach bandit. Another person who left his mark on this Midwest frontier was famous lawman "Wild" Bill Hickok. In 1876, Hickok played his last game of cards in Deadwood, South Dakota. Holding two pairs—aces and eights—in a poker game, he was shot in the back. Ever since, the hand has been known as a "Dead Man's Hand."

Some Black Hills towns had sizable populations of Chinese immigrants. Many had migrated to

California during the gold rush there and then moved to South Dakota when gold was found in those hills. The Chinese usually lived in their own neighborhoods and worked in laundries, stores, and mines. They also helped build the railroad lines that ran into the area.

In a few years time, the boom had turned to a bust. Before long, all the surface gold had been taken. Only big companies had the money to dig beneath the hills for gold underground. As the mining economy collapsed, people left the area as quickly as they had come. Many mining towns, including Tinton, Tigerville, Richford, and Cascade Springs, became ghost towns. A ghost town is an abandoned community where people no longer live. Other towns did survive, however, turning to farming, ranching, and lumbering to hold up their economies. Rapid City, founded in 1876 as a mining town, is today the second-largest town in South Dakota.

GHOST TOWNS IN THE BLACK HILLS

Today, the ruins of once-booming towns serve as reminders of the harsh life in the Black Hills. Some historians say that there are more than 400 ghost towns and ghost mines in South Dakota. Three of these towns are:

Spokane—Spokane was once home to more than 2,000 residents. The town formed around a mine that was known for its gold, zinc, and lead deposits. Today, a few buildings are still standing there, including the old schoolhouse.

Cascade Springs—Founded as a resort town in 1888, Cascade Springs attracted visitors with its warm mineral spring. The town was so popular that a four-story, 100-room hotel was built there. Unfortunately, the railroad bypassed the town, and by 1900, only a handful of people remained.

Medary—One of the first towns in the region, Medary was established in 1857. Raiding bands of Sioux warriors, however, soon convinced the townspeople to move their buildings to a larger town nearby. Today, little remains of Medary.

Martha Jane Canary (Calamity Jane) was given her nickname by a U.S. Calvary colonel whose life she saved during a battle with Indians in 1872.

CALAMITY JANE

Calamity Jane: Born Martha Jane Canary, this hard-living gunslinger and bullwhacker was said to have been raised by Midwest soldiers. A sharpshooter and a cardsharp, Jane claimed to have had a romance with Wild Bill Hickok. During a smallpox epidemic, she nursed many residents of Deadwood, South Dakota, back to health.

WILD WOMEN OF THE BLACK HILLS

The men who lived in the mining towns of the Black Hills could be rough and wild. Frontier women had to be tough, too. Here are a few of the womenfolk who were famous in the region.

Aunt Sally: The first nonnative woman in the Black Hills, Sarah Campbell was a cook for Lieutenant (loo-TEN-ant) Colonel Custer's 1874 military and mining expedition. Known as Aunt Sally, Campbell claimed one of the first mining stakes in the area. No one knows for sure whether she ever mined her claim. Aunt Sally died in 1888.

Poker Alice: Alice Tubbs was a gambler and card dealer in the mining town of Deadwood, South Dakota. Poker Alice sometimes earned $6,000 a night playing cards—plenty of cash to support her seven children. Charming and an elegant dresser, Alice also needed to be tough in the rough-and-tumble town. She always carried a gun and was not afraid to use it when she had to.

War for the Land

The Sioux people were upset and angry that their sacred hills, promised to them by U.S. treaty, were being invaded by white settlers. In 1875, conflict between the Sioux and Cheyenne people and the U.S. military heated up. The main leaders of the native resistance were Crazy Horse, a warrior chief of the Oglala Sioux; and Sitting Bull, a chief of the Hunkpapa Sioux.

Much of the fighting between the Native Americans and the U.S. military actually took place outside the Black Hills area. The most famous battle was the Battle of the Little Bighorn in June 1876. Custer and more than 250 of his men were wiped out by native warriors.

Four of Lieutenant Colonel George Armstrong Custer's six Crow Indian scouts pose for a photograph in 1908 among the tombstones on the battlefield at Little Bighorn, Montana.

Little Bighorn would be the final victory for the Sioux people. Inferior weapons and a lack of provisions led to their ultimate defeat. The remaining Sioux were forced onto reservations, areas set aside for them. Both of the great Sioux chiefs, Crazy Horse and Sitting Bull, were killed on the reservations.

Today

Tourism is an important part of the Black Hills economy. Area attractions include Custer State Park, Wind Cave National Park, and many ghost towns and ghost mines. One of the most popular tourist destinations is Mount Rushmore National Memorial. The memorial, which features the heads of four U.S. presidents carved into a tall granite cliff, attracts visitors from around the world. The presidents

FUN FACTS ABOUT
MOUNT RUSHMORE

- The sculpture on Mount Rushmore towers 500 feet (150 meters) above the valley floor. Each head is 60 feet (18 meters) tall.

- The memorial can be seen for more than 60 miles (96 kilometers).

- Begun in 1927, the entire project cost $1 million.

- Mount Rushmore National Memorial was created by American sculptor Gutzon Borglum. It was originally (oh-RIJ-ih-nal-ee) designed to show each president from the waist up.

- The first president to be completed was George Washington. The last, Roosevelt, was completed in 1941 by Lincoln Borglum after his father's death.

The faces of four presidents are carved in the granite of Mount Rushmore in South Dakota.

depicted are George Washington, Thomas Jefferson, Abraham Lincoln, and Theodore Roosevelt.

Seventeen miles (27 kilometers) from Mount Rushmore is the Crazy Horse Memorial. The monument, when finished, will be three-dimensional and more than 560 feet (168 meters) high. It will show the famous Sioux war chief upon his horse, pointing to his lands. Right now, only the face of the sculpture is finished.

Homestake Mine, the largest U.S. gold mine, is still in operation in Lead, South Dakota. The mine was purchased by millionaire George Hearst and opened in 1877. Over the years, it became the most productive gold mine in the nation. By 1901, the mine had produced more than $100 million in gold. Other minerals found in the hills include silver, copper, iron, and lead.

Great Lakes

2

The Great Lakes are five freshwater lakes located between the United States and Canada. Four of the lakes—Superior, Michigan (MISH-ih-gan), Huron, and Erie—are in the Midwest region. The fifth lake—Ontario—is located in the Northeast. Only Lake Michigan is completely within the United States. A smaller lake, Lake Saint Claire, is located on the eastern border of Michigan, near Detroit.

The lakes are connected to one another by rivers and canals. Together, the five lakes and Lake Saint Claire make up the largest body of freshwater in the world. They contain about nine-tenths of the nation's freshwater supply.

Since the 1700s, the lakes have played a major role in the history and growth of the United States. Used as a pathway for trade and travel for hundreds of years, the Great Lakes today make up one of the most important routes of inland commerce in the nation. The lakes are also a popular recreational and tourist destination.

Settlement

Geologically speaking, the Great Lakes are quite young. They were formed when huge, heavy Ice Age glaciers compressed the land millions of years ago, creating deep basins. When these glaciers began to melt about 11,000 years ago, the indentations filled with water, creating the Great Lakes.

Before the first Europeans arrived in the area, tribes of native peoples made their homes here. These groups included the Ojibwa (oh-JIB-wah), Fox, Potawatomi (PAHT-uh-waht-oh-mee), Huron, Winnebago (win-neh-BAY-goh), and Iroquois (IHR-uh-kwoy) peoples. The tribes hunted and fished. They also used the lakes to create extensive trade networks with one another, exchanging food, clothing, and furs. The native people used birch-bark canoes (kuh-NOOZ) to travel between the trading sites, which extended from what is now Minnesota all the way to New York.

GREAT LAKE STATS

How do the Great Lakes compare to one another? Check here and find out.

Lake	Erie	Huron	Michigan	Ontario	Superior
Length	241 miles (386 km.)	206 miles (330 km.)	307 miles (491 km.)	193 miles (309 km.)	350 miles (560 km.)
Maximum Width	57 miles (91 km.)	183 miles (293 km.)	118 miles (189 km.)	52 miles (83 km.)	160 miles (256 km.)
Area	9,940 sq. miles (25,844 sq. km.)	23,010 sq. miles (59,826 sq. km.)	22,400 sq. miles (58,240 sq. km.)	7,540 sq. miles (19,604 sq. km.)	31,820 sq. miles (82,732 sq. km.)
Average Depth	62 feet (19 meters)	195 feet (59 meters)	279 feet (84 meters)	283 feet (85 meters)	483 feet (145 meters)
Shoreline	871 miles (1,394 km.)	3,827 miles (6,123 km.)	1,638 miles (2,621 km.)	712 miles (1,139 km.)	2,726 miles (4,362 km.)

The earliest Europeans to explore the Great Lakes area were the French. One of the first was Étienne Brulé (AYT-yen broo-LAY), a scout for Samuel de Champlain. Champlain was a famous explorer who founded the first settlements in Canada for the French. Brulé was one of the first Europeans to see Lakes Huron, Ontario, and Superior. He spent many years living among the native people in the region, learning their languages and customs. Brulé was killed in 1632 by a group of hostile natives.

The French quickly took advantage of the wealth of natural resources in the area. They began trading with local tribes, exchanging guns, tools, and traps for animal pelts. The animal skins, especially (es-PESH-ul-ee) beaver, were shipped back east. Many other animals were trapped for their skins, including minks, wolves, and deer.

Trade with the native people of the area exploded in 1660. Soon, the French built a number of trading posts, forts, and missions. Many of the first area settlements had their starts as trading posts, including Cahokia, Illinois (il-ih-NOY); Sault Ste. Marie, Michigan; and Green Bay, Wisconsin.

EXPLORING THE GREAT LAKES

The first Europeans to explore the Great Lakes were the French. Because these vast, inland seas were so large, early adventurers believed they were looking at the Pacific (puh-SIFF-ik) Ocean.

Explorer	Country	Year	Lake Explored
Étienne Brûlé	France	1610	Huron
Samuel de Champlain	France	1615	Huron, Ontario
Étienne Brûlé	France	1622	Superior
Jean Nicolet	France	1634	Michigan
Louis Jolliet	France	1669	Erie

Struggle for Control
of the Lakes Region

Throughout the 1600s, France controlled the Midwest lakes region. Toward the end of the seventeenth century (SEN-chur-ee), however, England also claimed some of this region. Hostilities between the two countries grew, and in 1689, the first of four conflicts was fought. The final conflict, called the French and Indian War (1754–1763), ended with the British taking control of the lakes area east of the Mississippi. The British also took control of Canada in 1763.

After the American Revolution (1775–1783), the United States gained the Great Lakes area. Disputes over the exact boundaries between the United States and Canada caused more problems between the new country and Great Britain. Jay's Treaty in 1794 clarified the borders between the United States and Canada.

Great Britain was not about to let go of the profitable area without a struggle. When Jay's Treaty expired in 1805, problems quickly arose between Americans and British in the Great Lakes region. Quarrels over the area were one reason for the outbreak of the War of 1812 (1812–1815) in June of that year.

The Great Lakes were an important battle area during the war. Once war was declared, the British moved quickly to turn trading vessels into warships and take control of Lake Erie and Lake Ontario. Two months later, the British captured Detroit, Michigan. This gave them control of the Great Lakes area and access to the rest of the nation through its connecting waterways. Although the United States regained control of the Great Lakes by the end of the war, conflicts over the U.S.-Canadian border continued. Boundary issues between the two neighboring countries were finally resolved in 1818.

American naval officer Commodore Oliver Hazard Perry became a national hero after the battle of Lake Erie.

THE BATTLE OF LAKE ERIE

The only battle ever fought on a Great Lake was the Battle of Lake Erie during the War of 1812 (1812–1815). On September 10, 1813, Commodore Oliver Hazard Perry, commanding nine ships and 500 men, confronted the British fleet on Lake Erie. For hours, the fighting raged as the ships battled one another at close quarters. Finally, the British fleet surrendered. After the battle, Perry sent a message to General (JEN-er-ul) William Henry Harrison, commander of the Army of the Northwest and future U.S. president. The message said: "We have met the enemy and they are ours." In the upcoming weeks, the United States regained control of the Great Lakes area.

The Path to the West

After the opening of the Erie Canal in 1825, migration boomed. Thousands of settlers used the canal and the lakes as their pathway to the West. Thousands more stayed and made the lakes region their home. Some of the earliest immigrants to enter the lakes area were from Germany (JERM-an-ee), Poland, Finland, Sweden, Greece, Italy, Ireland, and Russia.

After the Civil War (1861–1865), these immigrants provided the labor for the many industries that quickly grew in the area. They worked at steel mills, coal mines, slaughterhouses (SLAW-ter-how-sez), and docks. They fueled the population growth of cities like Milwaukee, Wisconsin; Chicago, Illinois; and Cleveland, Ohio.

Living conditions for the immigrants were poor. They lived in the worst neighborhoods and performed the dirtiest, most dangerous jobs for low wages. A Chicago resident, Jane Addams, wanted to change that. In 1889, she founded Hull House in an immigrant neighborhood. Hull House provided such services as English classes, parenting classes, and recreational activities for children. Soon, Addams's settlement house was being copied in cities throughout the country.

Jane Addams talks with a group of young people who are visiting Hull House in Chicago, Illinois in 1935.

LAKE SUPERIOR

The Coast Guard cutter Mackinaw clears a path through the ice of Lake Superior.

- Superior is the largest of the Great Lakes.
- It is the largest freshwater lake in the world.
- It is the northernmost, westernmost, coldest, and deepest of the Great Lakes.
- Important Midwest lake ports include Duluth, Minnesota; Marquette, Michigan (MISH-ih-gan); and Ashland, Wisconsin.
- The Ojibwa (oh-JIB-wah) people called the lake *kitchi gami*, meaning "great lake." Early French explorers named the lake *Le Lac Superieur*, meaning "Upper Lake."

Travel and Commerce on the Lakes

From the earliest days of European settlement around the Great Lakes, trade and shipping have been the most important industries. Even before the French arrived in the early 1600s, Native American tribes had developed trade networks throughout the region.

The first commodity to be shipped out of the area was furs. The Great Lakes area is rich in other natural resources, as well, and it wasn't long before settlers realized this. In the 1800s, plenty of lumber, iron, copper, coal, and limestone were all found near the Great Lakes.

As trade became more important to the area's economy, people realized that safe and convenient routes between the lakes and other waterways needed to be created. Some of the rivers connecting the lakes were impossible to travel because of rapids, waterfalls, or shallow sections. Traders were forced to haul their boats overland for part of the trips between the lakes.

In addition, the lakes are not all at the same elevation. The Great Lakes are like a stairway that descends from west to east. Lake Superior, the westernmost lake, is the highest step. These differences in elevation also added to the difficulty of getting from one lake to another by boat. Something needed to be done to help the region grow to its full potential (poh-TEN-chul).

Canals and Locks

As early as the 1700s, people realized the need for canals to make travel between the lakes easier. However, support and money was not available until the early 1800s. One of the first canals to make a difference to Great Lakes trade was the Erie Canal, finished in 1825. The Erie Canal connected Lake Erie to the Atlantic coast via the Hudson River. However, the canal was not large enough for travel by oceangoing vessels.

In 1855, the first of three Sault Ste. Marie Canals opened up between Lake Huron and Lake Superior. The new canal allowed ships to travel directly between these two lakes, avoiding the rapids in between. The new canal helped make Duluth, Minnesota, a bustling port. By the 1890s, millions of tons of iron were being sent through the canal from mines in the west to points east.

Eventually, four locks were also built in the canal. Locks are enclosed areas where the water level can be lowered or raised to allow ships to pass between bodies of water that are at different elevations. For example, a boat leaving Lake Superior would wait in a lock until the water level in the lock had been lowered to Lake Huron's level. Then it could continue on its way.

The waterway that had the most impact on the Great Lakes shipping industry was the St. Lawrence Seaway. The United States and Canada began working together on the seaway in 1954. Completed five years later, the deepwater pathway opened the Great Lakes and the St. Lawrence River to large, oceangoing ships. It provided a direct route to the Atlantic for the big boats. Today, a ship can sail from the Gulf of St. Lawrence all the way to Duluth, the westernmost port on the lakes. The one-way voyage is more than 2,340 miles (3,744 kilometers).

SPANNING THE LAKES

Before 1957, people who wanted to travel between Michigan's Upper and Lower Peninsulas had to find a way to cross the Mackinac (MAK-ih-naw) Straits between Lakes Huron and Michigan. That changed when the Mackinac Bridge opened for business. Known by area residents as the "Mighty Mac," the bridge is one of the longest suspension bridges in the world. It measures more than 8,600 feet (2,580 meters) in length and towers 150 feet (45 meters) above the water.

LAKE HURON

A fisherman enjoys a quiet day on Lake Huron.

- Huron is the second largest of the Great Lakes.

- Its 30,000 islands help give it the longest shoreline of the Great Lakes.

- Manitoulin (man-uh-TOO-lin) Island in the lake is the world's largest island in a freshwater lake.

- Important Midwest lake ports include Port Huron and Bay City.

- The lake was named by French explorers after the Huron tribe who lived on its banks. Other early French adventurers called it the Sweet Sea.

LAKE MICHIGAN

The South Haven, Michigan, pier and lighthouse are engulfed in mist and water from Lake Michigan as a near hurricane force storm crashes ashore.

- Michigan is the third largest of the Great Lakes.

- It is the only Great Lake that is entirely within the United States.

- The world's largest freshwater sand dunes are on the lake's shorelines.

- Important Midwest lake ports include Green Bay and Milwaukee, Wisconsin; Chicago, Illinois; Gary, Indiana; and Sheboygan, Wisconsin.

- Native peoples called the lake *michi gami*, meaning "large lake." Some early French explorers called it the Lake of the Stinking Water.

LAKE DANGERS

The Great Lakes can be a sailor's nightmare. Sudden storms, savage winds and waves, and bitterly cold winter temperatures all make sailing the lakes as risky as sailing the oceans. The very first ship to sail the lakes, the *Griffon*, was also the first ship to learn of the dangers. In 1679, the ship disappeared without a trace after leaving Green Bay, Wisconsin. Since then, more than 4,200 ships have been lost on the lakes, along with the thousands of people who sailed on them. The worst lake disaster occurred in 1915, when the excursion steamer *Eastland* rolled over at its mooring. More than 800 people died within a few feet of the Chicago shore. One of the most famous Great Lakes disasters was the wreck of the *Edmund Fitzgerald* (fitz-JERR-uld) in 1975. The gigantic freighter (FRAY-terz), carrying a heavy load of iron ore, sank in a fierce winter storm. Twenty-nine men lost their lives when the ship went down.

Trade Takes Off

By the 1880s, locks, canals, and channels were helping Great Lakes port cities to thrive. Raw materials, including grain, iron, coal, and lumber, were shipped east, while finished products were shipped west to the Great Lakes. During the 1890s, Chicago was the fourth-busiest port in the world despite being closed four months out of each year during the winter.

The demand for goods from the area, along with the availability of an excellent (EK-sell-ent) shipping route, helped business boom in the Great Lakes region. Soon, factories, refineries, and mills were popping up all around the lakes. The Calumet (KAL-yuh-met) region in Indiana, for example, became an important area for iron, steel, and chemical (KEM-ik-ul) processing.

The natural resources of the area became especially important during World War II (1939–1945), when steel from the Great Lakes was used to build airplanes, ships, and weapons. Steel is still an important cargo on the Great Lakes. Steel, iron, coal, and grain make up about 80 percent of all cargo shipped over the lakes.

Today, thanks to the St. Lawrence Seaway, the Great Lakes are home to fifteen international ports. Ships from more than fifty nations, as well as from U.S. and Canadian fleets, ply the waters. These boats include giant freighters (FRAY-terz), tow-barges, and huge oceangoing vessels nicknamed "salties."

These ships carry more than 100 million tons (90 million metric tons) of cargo each year.

• Fast Fact •
The biggest boat to ever sail the Great Lakes is the *Paul R. Tregurtha*. It measures more than 1,000 feet (300 meters) in length—longer than three football fields.

Today

Tourism on the Great Lakes has skyrocketed over the past few years. In the summertime, people visit lakeside beaches to swim, sail, and enjoy the sunshine. Another popular summer activity is scuba diving. Divers can explore some of the many shipwrecks that lie at the bottom of the lakes. During the winter, as well, the Great Lakes are a place for fun and excitement. Ice fishing, skiing, and snowmobiling all contribute to the region's appeal.

There are also a number of national parks in the Great Lakes area that attract thousands of tourists every year. These parks include Sleeping Bear Dunes National Seashore along Lake Michigan and Isle Royale National Park along Lake Superior. Those who want to visit Isle Royale must take a boat or a seaplane. Tourists interested in the area's seafaring history can visit one of several maritime museums that dot the lakes' shores.

LAKE ERIE

A lone kayaker makes his way past a lighthouse on Lake Erie near Cleveland, Ohio.

- Erie is the fourth largest of the Great Lakes.

- It is the southernmost and warmest of the Great Lakes.

- Because it is the shallowest of all the Great Lakes, Erie is the only one that completely freezes over during the winter.

- Important Midwest lake ports include Cleveland, Toledo, and Ashtabula, all in Ohio.

- Like Lake Huron, Erie was named for a tribe of native people living near its shore.

Other people come to the Great Lakes to visit one of the big cities in the region. Three big cities that attract visitors include Chicago, Illinois, on Lake Michigan; Cleveland, Ohio, on Lake Erie; and Milwaukee, Wisconsin, on Lake Michigan. All three cities are filled with fun and fascinating things to do.

Sports fans flock to the area to watch their favorite professional sports teams play. Professional teams in the Great Lakes region include the Chicago Cubs and White Sox, Cleveland Indians, Detroit Tigers, and Milwaukee Brewers (baseball); the Chicago Bulls, Cleveland Cavaliers, Detroit Pistons, and Milwaukee Bucks (basketball); the Chicago Bears, Cleveland Browns, Detroit Lions, and Green Bay Packers (football); and the Chicago Blackhawks and Detroit Red Wings (hockey).

Pollution Problems

More people and businesses near the Great Lakes have led to more pollution around the region and in the lakes themselves. Sewage, pesticides (PESS-tih-sydez), dirt, and acid rain have affected all of the lakes to some degree. In Lake Erie, for example, recent fish kills puzzled scientists. In 2001, some of Lake Huron's beaches had to be closed because bacterial levels were too high. Today, more than forty areas around the Great Lakes are badly polluted and require immediate attention.

Nonnative species (SPEE-sheez) are another problem in the Great Lakes. This problem is due to improved access to the lakes. One nonnative creature in the lakes is the sea lamprey, an eel-like fish that has nearly wiped out lake trout in Lakes Huron and Michigan. The sea lamprey may have entered the lakes through the St. Lawrence Seaway. The zebra mussel is another troublesome creature that does not belong in the lakes. Brought by oceangoing ships in

LAKE ONTARIO

The Toronto, Canada skyline is visible behind this ferry as it sails the waters of Lake Ontario.

- Ontario is the smallest of the Great Lakes.

- It is the only Great Lake that is located completely outside the Midwest.

- Lake Ontario is the most polluted of all the Great Lakes.

- Important Ontario lake ports include Oswego and Rochester in New York and Kingston and Toronto in Ontario, Canada.

- The lake was first explored by Étienne Brulé (AYT-yen broo-LAY) and Samuel de Champlain in 1615. First called *Lac St. Louis* by the French, the lake was later renamed *Ontario*, an Iroquois (IHR-uh-kwoy) word meaning "beautiful lake."

1985 or 1986, the mussels coat any hard surfaces, including boat hulls and engines, and clog water intake pipes at power plants. They have also reduced the populations of native mussels in the area.

People in the Great Lakes region are working together to clean up these natural treasures. Both the United States and Canada share the lakes, so cooperative efforts by both countries are important. Because the Great Lakes are interconnected, the health of one lake affects the health of all of the others. One of the earliest international agreements between the two countries was the 1909 Boundary Waters Treaty. In 1972, the two nations signed the Great Lakes Water Quality Agreement. Both treaties are agreements on how the two nations will share control and care of the Great Lakes.

Efforts are also underway to control populations of nonnative species. In 1990, the Nonindigenous (non-in-DIH-jin-us) Aquatic Nuisance (NOO-sense) Act was passed by the U.S. Congress. This act provides for research to stop the spread of zebra mussels and other nonnative animals.

Great Plains

3

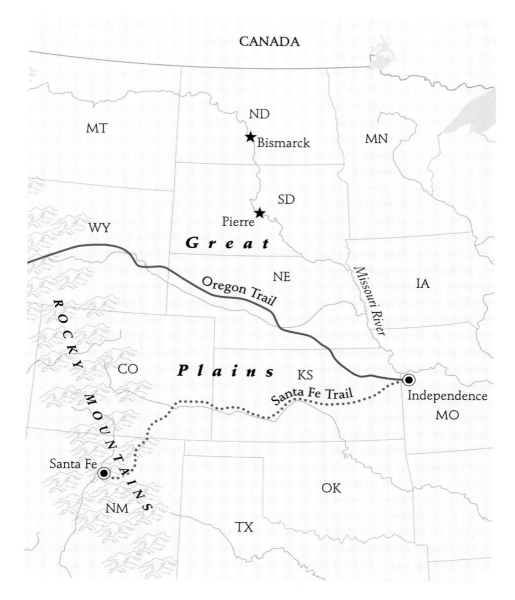

The Great Plains are an immense grassy region that extends more than 2,500 miles (4,000 kilometers) from Canada in the north to Texas in the south. The western border of the Great Plains is the Rocky Mountains. The eastern border is near the 100th meridian of longitude (LAWN-jih-tood). The width of the Great Plains varies, from 300 miles (480 kilometers) in some areas to 700 miles (1,120 kilometers) in others. These vast, rolling grasslands stretch through parts of the Midwest states of North Dakota, South Dakota, Nebraska, and Kansas, as well as some Western and Southwestern states.

The Great Plains region is semiarid, which means that it receives less than average rainfall each year. Generally (JEN-er-ul-lee), less than 20 inches (50 centimeters) of rain falls in the area each year. (The Southeast, in contrast, receives twice that amount of rain.) The plains are also subject to weather extremes, from blizzards and bitterly cold temperatures in the winter to dust storms, tornadoes, and frequent thunderstorms in the summer.

Over the years, the Great Plains have helped shape the nation's history. Since the mid-1800s, pioneers have traveled through and settled in the area, forging a new life for themselves on the American frontier. The plains have also played an important role in our nation's growing economy. The region is an important agricultural area. Where water is available, the soil is fertile and good for farming. Grasses for grazing cattle and other livestock are plentiful. The area is also known for its mineral wealth.

THE 100TH MERIDIAN

The 100th meridian of longitude (LAWN-jih-tood) is an imaginary line that begins at the North Pole and runs south through the center of the United States to the South Pole. In the late 1800s, American surveyors noticed that west of the 100th meridian, lands were arid and received less than 20 inches (50 centimeters) of rainfall and snowfall, or *precipitation* (pruh-sip-ih-TAY-shun), each year. For this reason, the meridian is sometimes known as the "rainfall line" or the "twenty-inch line." East of the meridian, the climate is more humid, and crops can be grown more easily. The meridian serves as the easternmost boundary of the Great Plains.

Settlement

The first people to live on the Great Plains were ancestors (AN-sess-terz) of Native Americans. These early plains dwellers migrated to the region from Asia as early as 25,000 years ago. Centuries (SEN-chur-eez) later, many tribes of Native Americans lived in the region. These tribes included the Sioux (SOO), Pawnee, and Cheyenne (shye-ANN).

Although the Plains natives spoke many different languages, they were united by their way of life. Most tribes were nomadic, following the trails of the huge herds of bison, or buffalo, that roamed the plains. The native peoples of the plains relied on the buffalo for food, clothing, and shelter. While on the trail, the natives lived in tepees, cone-shaped dwellings made of wooden poles and covered with buffalo skin. The tepees could be easily taken down and set up again at the next campsite. Even dried buffalo manure, called "buffalo chips," was used as fuel by the Plains tribes.

European Arrival

The first Europeans to explore the plains were Spanish conquistadors. Conquistador (kohn-KEES-tah-dor) is the Spanish word for "conqueror." The first Spanish expedition into the region was led by Francisco Vásquez (fran-SISS-koh VAHS-kez) de Coronado in 1541. In search of gold and other riches, Coronado was not at all impressed with the area. He advised his superiors to avoid establishing any settlements there.

Coronado and other Spanish explorers left a permanent mark on the plains: the horse. Abandoned or escaped mustangs, brought from Europe by the Spaniards, would eventually change the culture of the Plains tribes. The tribes became more warlike, using the horses to hunt and wage war on other tribes.

French explorer La Salle claimed to have discovered the Ohio River and appropriated the Louisiana region for France. La Salle was murdered by his men in 1687.

In 1682, French explorer René-Robert Cavelier (kav-ul-YAY), sieur (lord) de La Salle, claimed the region as part of the Louisiana Territory for France. In the 1700s, French adventurers began exploring the plains region. The French set up trading posts where they bartered with the native people in the area, exchanging guns, alcohol, and trinkets for beaver, deer, and buffalo pelts.

EARLY PLAINS EXPLORERS

The first Great Plains explorers were Spanish and French. Only after the Louisiana Purchase in 1803 did Americans really begin surveying their new territory.

Explorer	Country	Year	Area Explored
Francisco Vásquez de Coronado	Spain	1541	Kansas
Pierre Gaultier de Varennes, sieur de la Vérendrye	France	1738	North Dakota
Pierre and Paul Mallet	France	1739	Nebraska
François and Louis-Joseph Gaultier de la Vérendrye	France	1743	South Dakota
Meriwether Lewis and William Clark	United States	1804	Missouri River and Great Plains

In 1803, the United States bought a large chunk of land from France that included the Great Plains. The Louisiana Purchase, as the sale was called, more than doubled the size of the nation. At first, the only interest in the new territory west of the Mississippi was as a source of furs and as a place to resettle Native American tribes from the East. For American politicians (pahl-uh-TISH-anz), who believed that no Americans would want to settle in the arid region, the Great Plains seemed the perfect place to relocate the eastern tribes.

• *Fast Fact* •
In 1820, army surveyor Stephen Long dubbed the Great Plains "the Great American Desert."

The Overland Trails

The first pioneers who entered the Great Plains from the East were not interested in settling there. These people were just passing through the plains on their way westward. They traveled in prairie schooners, wagons covered with white canvas, using the overland trails that wound through the prairies and plains and across the mountains. Prairie schooners, lighter than other covered wagons, were pulled by up to four horses or oxen, large farm animals related to cows.

The journey through the plains was difficult. Pioneers faced hostile Native Americans, disease, accidents, and other hardships. Many settlers died before ever reaching their destinations. The journey west was particularly hard for children and the elderly.

One of the first overland trails that opened up through the plains was the Santa Fe Trail. A trader named William Becknell first blazed the trail in 1821. Settlers began their trips in Franklin, Missouri, and traveled through the Great Plains of Kansas before reaching Santa Fe, New Mexico. The entire journey was about 780 miles (1,248 kilometers) and took as long as two months to complete. A major trade and settlement route, the plains trail was traveled by as many as 5,000 wagons each year.

Another famous overland trail that cut across the plains was the Oregon Trail. The trail was first mapped in 1842 by the U.S. Army. Kit Carson, a famous trapper and mountain man, helped blaze the route. In the mid-1800s, the Oregon Trail was the most widely used pathway to the West. From Independence (in-duh-PEN-dense), Missouri, the trail followed the Platte River through the Great Plains of Nebraska. From here, settlers made their way across the Rocky Mountains and on to the Oregon Territory. The 2,000-mile (3,200-kilometer) trip took about six months to complete.

Chimney Rock was the most famous landmark along the Oregon Trail. It could be seen several days before pioneers traveling the trail arrived at its base.

As more and more people traveled the overland trails from East to West, forts, military and trading posts, and towns sprang up along the way. The forts and military posts were built to protect migrating people from attacking native tribes. The trading posts and towns were established to make the journey a little easier. Before long, people began eyeing the plains as a destination.

FEBOLD FEBOLDSON

Febold Feboldson is a fictional character, the Paul Bunyan of the Great Plains. Feboldson was the creation of a Great Plains newspaper in the 1920s. He was the hero of many tall tales about the last frontier and its early settlers. One yarn spun about the big Swedish farmer told how he created a perfectly straight border between the Kansas and Nebraska territories. Over several years, Feboldson bred bees with eagles until he had a really big bee. He then hitched the bee to a plow and had it draw a beeline between the two territories.

Homesteaders Hit the Plains

For many years, the idea that the Great Plains were a desert wasteland kept settlers away. They were more than happy to think of the region as part of Indian Territory. But in the 1840s, people in search of fertile—and cheap—farmland began making their homes on the plains.

In 1854, the U.S. government passed the Kansas-Nebraska Act, which allowed settlers in a large area of the plains. Then in 1862, the Homestead Act was passed. Under this act, each family that settled in the Great Plains would receive 160 acres (64 hectares) of public land—provided that they worked part of the land and stayed for five years. Settlers who took advantage of the new law were dubbed "homesteaders."

The life of a homesteading family was difficult. Many of the first plains pioneers lived in sod houses, built out of squares of dirt cut from the earth. These sod homes were dirty and dark. Because they settled on such large plots of land, families were far away from other homesteaders. The settlers also had to learn to deal with the wild weather on the plains. Blizzards, tornadoes, droughts (DROWTZ), and grasshopper plagues were all part of the plains way of life.

This Nebraska sod house is typical of those built by early settlers on the Great Plains.

After the Civil War (1861–1865), many former slaves from the South migrated to the plains. Called "exodusters," these settlers were looking for the economic opportunities that they could not get in the South. The Great Plains of Kansas and Nebraska were major destinations for the exodusters.

The Indian Wars

As more and more settlers arrived on the Great Plains, Native American tribes were pushed off their land. The U.S. government forced them onto reservations, areas set aside for the Native Americans. Many of the reservations were located in undesirable areas, on land that no white settlers were interested in.

Some of the tribes were not about to give up their lands and go to the reservations without a fight. In the 1850s, battles between U.S. troops and some tribes, especially (es-PESH-ul-ee) the Sioux and Cheyenne, broke out. Although the Civil War temporarily focused the U.S. government's attention away from the plains frontier, the conflict heated up once the war had ended. Army troops, as well as volunteer forces of "Indian fighters," began an all-out effort to herd the remaining Native Americans of the Great Plains onto reservations.

The Sioux and Cheyenne had many brave war chiefs to lead them. These leaders included Sitting Bull of the Lakota Sioux and Red Cloud and Crazy Horse of the Oglala Sioux. Despite their fierce determination to hold onto their land, the tribes were no match for the cannons and other weapons of the U.S. Army.

The last armed battle between the remaining Plains tribes and the U.S. Army was at Wounded Knee, South Dakota, in 1890. In December, Sitting Bull was killed at the Pine Ridge Sioux Reservation in South Dakota as army troops tried to arrest him. Many of Sitting Bull's followers fled. They were pursued to the camp of Chief Big Foot near Wounded Knee Creek. On December 29, the army wiped out Big Foot and his band of Sioux. As many as 370 men, women, and children—most of them innocent bystanders—were killed.

The Lakota Sioux chief, Sitting Bull, is shown in this nineteenth-century photograph.

DODGE CITY: HELL ON THE PLAINS

In 1872, a small town was founded along the Santa Fe Trail to serve buffalo hunters, traders, and cowboys. Although it began as a one-building town, Dodge City quickly grew. Before long, the town had a general (JEN-er-ul) store, nineteen saloons, and an evil reputation. Known as the "wickedest little city in America," Dodge City was the site of shootings, brawls, and drunken behavior. Wyatt Earp, Bat Masterson, and Doc Holliday all made names for themselves as lawmen who tried to keep the wild town under control. Visitors to Dodge City today can still see Boot Hill, a cemetery (SEM-ih-tehr-ee) where the losers of gun battles were buried.

Railroads Open the Plains

In 1862, the U.S. Congress set the stage for an event that would open up the Great Plains to settlers, traders, and adventurers alike. That year, Congress agreed to give 100 million acres (40 million hectares) of land to railroad companies that would build a railway from the Atlantic coast to the Pacific (puh-SIFF-ik) coast. Two companies took the challenge, and three years later, the first sections of a transcontinental railway were laid.

In 1863, the Central Pacific began building an eastward-bound railway from Sacramento, California. Two years later, the Union Pacific Railroad began laying down track in Omaha, Nebraska, one of the westernmost points for railroads from the East. Eventually, the two railroads would meet and connect in Promontory Summit, Utah, creating the first transcontinental railroad.

The Union Pacific hired Civil War veterans and Irish immigrants to build the tracks that would cross the Great Plains. The men worked feverishly, braving attacks by Native Americans and the extreme

weather of the region. By the time they reached *Railroad officials* Utah, the laborers had laid more than 1,000 miles *and employees celebrate the* (1,600 kilometers) of track. *completion of*

The two railroads were connected in 1869, and the *the first* transcontinental railroad went into operation. Travelers *transcontinental railroad in* could now make the trip from one coast of the United *Promontory, Utah.* States to the other in about eight days. Before the railroad, the trip took more than six months.

The 1870s saw a boom in immigration to the area as settlers began to use this new mode of transportation. The number of towns, farms, and ranches along the railroad lines quickly grew. As traffic on the railways increased, the Santa Fe and Oregon Trails fell into disuse.

A protected bison herd grazes in Theodore Roosevelt National Park in North Dakota. About 500 buffalo live in the park.

THE LAST OF THE BUFFALO

For the Great Plains tribes, one of the most devastating events of the nineteenth century (SEN-chur-ee) was the destruction of the herds of buffalo that roamed the region. The tribes counted on the buffalo for food, shelter, and clothing. However, the pioneers moving onto the plains wanted to get rid of these creatures. Buffalo competed with cattle for valuable grazing space. In addition, the federal government knew that wiping out the buffalo would take away the native peoples' means of survival. In the 1860s, millions of buffalo roamed the Great Plains. By 1880, only a small number of the animals remained.

Economy

In the 1860s, ranching became the first major business of the Great Plains. Cattle owners from Texas, driving their herds to the railway lines in Abilene (AB-ih-leen), Kansas, found that the grass-covered plains were perfect for grazing their herds. With the invention of barbed wire in the early 1870s, ranchers could fence off large tracts of lands, claiming the areas as their own. Barbed wire, developed by an

Illinois (il-ih-NOY) farmer, provided an inexpensive method of fencing. By the 1880s, the fences could be found everywhere over the plains.

The 1880s were a time of trouble for plains ranchers. In 1886 and 1887, fierce blizzards raged over the region. One storm in 1887 lasted for seventy-two hours. During the blizzards, some families froze to death. Millions of cattle died, and many ranchers went bankrupt.

Despite the hard times, ranching quickly made a comeback on the Great Plains. Soon, millions of cattle roamed the plains. Ranching is still going strong in the plains region today. Cattle, goats, and sheep are some of the livestock that roam this Midwest area.

Farmers on the Plains

With the building of a transcontinental railroad, thousands of people flocked to the Great Plains. Most of them turned to grain farming to make a living. The plains area attracted immigrants from Norway, Sweden, Germany (JERM-an-ee), and France. These pioneers quickly learned that farming on the Plains— with annual rainfall and snowfall, or precipitation (pruh-sip-ih-TAY-shun), of about 20 inches (50 centimeters)—was going to take a special effort.

Plains farmers soon perfected the method of dry farming. Dry farming is the frequent plowing of the

THE CATTLE DRIVE

Beginning in the 1860s, ranchers from Texas drove their longhorn cattle to such Great Plains cities as Abilene (AB-ih-leen) and Dodge City, Kansas. Here, the cattle were herded into railroad cars and shipped east to slaughterhouses (SLAW-ter-how-sez) and processing plants in Chicago, Illinois (il-ih-NOY). Cattle drives could take a month or longer. Cowboys herded large numbers of the animals along the dusty dirt trails, fending off bands of hostile Native Americans and cattle rustlers. At the end of the trail, they could spend their hard-earned money in the saloons and gambling parlors of Dodge City.

soil to keep it moist. They also found a number of ways to irrigate their fields, including using windmills to pump water. The invention of steel-tipped plows to cut easily through the soil also helped plains farmers.

The population of the Great Plains depended upon the weather. When rain was plentiful, people flocked into the area to farm the fertile grasslands. In times of drought, things were different. In 1886, for example, a decade-long drought began. Crops failed, and thousands of people who had tried to make a living on the land left the area. To make matters worse, many farmers believed the old saying that "rain follows the plow"; they thought that if they kept plowing, the rain would come. This led to overplowing, a practice that damaged the soil for years to come.

This cloud of top soil parched by drought and picked up by winds moves down a road near Boise City, Oklahoma in 1935.

The worst drought in recent history began in the early 1930s. For years, poor farming practices such as overcropping and overplowing had eroded the plains topsoil. With no rain to add moisture to the soil, blowing dust and dirt soon covered buildings, cars, and animals. The dust storms became known as "black blizzards." Thousands of people were forced out of the region. Areas of the plains that were hit the worst earned the nickname of "the Dust Bowl."

In recent years, improved farming practices have helped ensure that a disaster like the 1930s drought does not occur again. Today, the Great Plains are the top grain-producing region in the United States. Wheat, alfalfa, barley, oats, rye, and corn are all grown here.

THE RANGE WARS

As farmers and ranchers settled side by side on the Great Plains, problems arose. Ranchers wanted large expanses of land for themselves. They needed the land for their herds of cattle to graze. To protect the open lands that they used, some ranchers fenced off property that was not even theirs. The farmers protested. Why should the ranchers be entitled to the best farmland?

Farmers formed secret societies (suh-SYE-uh-teez) to cut down the fences and burn grazing lands. Ranchers hired gangs of armed thugs to scare off the farmers. Sometimes, people were killed during the confrontations. In the 1880s, the two groups were forced to work together to face common enemies: droughts (DROWTZ) and blizzards.

Mining and Manufacturing

In the early 1900s, yet another resource was discovered in the Great Plains: mineral wealth. One of the first minerals found on the plains was gold. The 1874 discovery in the Black Hills of South Dakota set off a gold rush to the area that would displace the Sioux from their reservation. Later, oil, coal, natural gas, iron, and uranium all became important parts of the region's economy, especially after World War II (1941–1945).

In recent years, manufacturing has become much more important to the Great Plains economy. Factories that make food products, electronics, machinery (muh-SHEEN-er-ee), and many other items all contribute to the wealth of the region.

Today

In recent years, the Great Plains have experienced (ex-PEER-ee-enst) a decline in population, as people move away from the farming towns and into larger cities. Currently, only about 2 percent of the U.S. population lives on the Great Plains, a region that covers about 20 percent of the nation. Although the number of people on the plains is declining, the number of buffalo, once almost extinct in the region, is growing. Today, there are thousands of bison on the plains. The number has grown as ranchers become interested in raising buffalo, which are used as an alternate source of meat.

Many people are working to preserve the vast grasslands. Programs that set aside parts of the plains as parks and preserves are returning these lands to their former state. Farmers today are also more aware of the effects of agriculture on the land around them. Many of them now farm in a way that conserves the plains' most valuable resource: the land. Conservationists hope that plants and grasses, as well as the birds and other species (SPEE-sheez) that depend upon them, will make a comeback, thanks to these and other efforts.

Mississippi River

4

The Mississippi River is the nation's most important waterway. From the early 1800s, the upper river has played a key role in the development of our nation, economically and socially. For thousands of years, people have used the river as a means of exploration and transportation. Settlers used the river and its tributaries to travel from the eastern United States to the west.

The Mississippi has its source in Lake Itasca in northwest Minnesota. From here, it winds through ten states to the Mississippi Delta in the Gulf of

Mexico. The delta is a large area of land formed by the buildup of sand, soil, and other river deposits. In all, the river travels 2,348 miles (3,757 kilometers), twisting and turning all the way.

The upper Mississippi runs through five Midwest states: Minnesota, Wisconsin, Iowa, Illinois (il-ih-NOY), and Missouri. The river serves as the eastern boundary of most of Missouri, all of Iowa, and part of Minnesota. It follows the western border of Illinois and part of Wisconsin. The landscape of the upper Mississippi is very different from the lower part. The upper section flows down steep waterfalls, through high cliffs, and past hundreds of small islands. As it moves further south, it winds its way through hills, prairies, and some of the richest farmland in the nation.

More than 250 tributaries, smaller rivers or streams, flow into the Mississippi. The Missouri River, which enters the Mississippi just north of St. Louis, is the river's largest tributary. Other major tributaries in the Midwest include the Ohio, Wisconsin, and Illinois Rivers. The Mississippi drains more than 1.2 million square miles (3.1 million square kilometers) between the Rockies and the Alleghenies (al-uh-GAY-neez), carrying rainwater and melted snow to the Gulf of Mexico.

MISSISSIPPI MEASUREMENTS

Here's how the Mississippi compares to some other U.S. rivers.

River	Length
Mississippi	2,348 miles (3,757 kilometers)
Missouri	2,714 miles (4,342 kilometers)
Rio Grande	1,885 miles (3,016 kilometers)
Arkansas	1,396 miles (2,234 kilometers)
Snake	1,083 miles (1,733 kilometers)
Red	1,018 miles (1,629 kilometers)
Connecticut	410 miles (656 kilometers)

Settlement

The Mississippi was formed about 10,000 years ago. Melting glaciers carved the twisting, turning channels that would become the big river and its many tributaries. Soon after, humans settled around the river. One group of early native people was known as the Mound Builders. These early people used large dirt mounds as burial and ceremonial (sehr-uh-MOH-nee-al) sites. In some groups, leaders or respected members lived in homes built on platforms on top of large mounds.

Tourists view Monks Mound at the Cahokia Mounds State Historic Site in Collinsville, Illinois. The mound was once the spiritual and political center for a community of more than 20,000 Mississippian Indians.

Cahokia State Historic Site is located across the Mississippi River from St. Louis. Cahokia is a 2,000-acre (800-hectare) site that contains a number of ancient mounds. The largest, Monks Mound, covers 14 acres (5.6 hectares) and towers 100 feet (30 meters) above the ground. Monks Mound may have been used as a platform upon which several buildings were raised. Cahokia was first inhabited around A.D. 700. About 100 years before Europeans arrived in the area, however, the Cahokia Mound Builders disappeared.

When the first Europeans began visiting the upper Mississippi, several Native American tribes lived along the river's banks. These tribes included the Ojibwa (oh-JIB-wah), Sauk, Fox, and Sioux (SOO). Many of the tribes planted crops in the fertile soil surrounding the river. They also fished in the river and hunted in nearby forests. Native Americans gave the river its name. They called it messipi, meaning "big water," and also mee-zee-see-bee, meaning "father of the waters."

THE SEARCH FOR THE SOURCE

In 1832, geologist Henry Schoolcraft set out in search of the source of the Mississippi River. Schoolcraft consulted the native peoples of the area, who guided him to a small lake in Minnesota. Schoolcraft named the body of water Lake Itasca by combining the Latin words veritas ("true") and caput ("head"). At Lake Itasca, the mighty Mississippi begins as a small stream about 12 feet (3.6 meters) wide and just 4 inches (10 centimeters) deep. In 1933, a bridge of stepping stones was created across the stream. Visitors to the Mississippi headwaters can use the stepping stones to walk across the river here.

The Jesuit priest Father Jacques Marquette explored the Mississippi River from the Great Lakes to Arkansas.

European Exploration

The French were the first Europeans to explore the upper Mississippi. In 1673, Father Jacques Marquette and Louis Jolliet set out from New France—now Canada—to the Great Lakes. From there, they journeyed to the Mississippi River. The two men were in search of the Northwest Passage to the Pacific (puh-SIFF-ik) Ocean. They traveled downstream as far as Arkansas (AR-ken-saw) before turning back.

In 1680, René-Robert Cavelier (kav-ul-YAY), sieur (lord) de La Salle, sent Father Louis Hennepin to explore the area around the upper Mississippi more thoroughly. During his expedition, Hennepin discovered that powerful waterfalls blocked the way north. He named the raging waters, located near what

is now Minneapolis (minn-ee-APP-oh-liss)–St. Paul,
Minnesota—the Falls of St. Anthony. Two years later,
La Salle himself traveled the entire course of the
Mississippi, claiming the river basin for France. La
Salle named France's new territory Louisiana after the
French king Louis XIV.

As the French explored the upper Mississippi, they
set up trading posts and fortresses along the big river's
banks. Many trading posts would later grow into the
region's biggest, most important cities, such as St.
Louis, Missouri; St. Paul, Minnesota; and Prairie du
Chien, Wisconsin.

After the American Revolution (1775–1783) ended,
the United States took control of nearly all the land
east of the Mississippi. (Florida was the only
exception.) Twenty years later, President Thomas
Jefferson bought the huge area west of the river that
belonged to France. The Louisiana Purchase, as the sale
is known, doubled the size of the United States and
ended all foreign (FOHR-in) control of the Mississippi.

Gateway to the West

After the Louisiana Purchase, the Mississippi and its
tributaries became the chief highways for western
settlement. Pioneers and traders flowed into the
Mississippi area. They used the river ports as
jumping-off spots for their journeys to the west.
Many people decided to settle by the Mississippi,
attracted by the wealth of natural resources along the
big river.

One Mississippi River city in particular would earn
the title "Gateway to the West": St. Louis, Missouri.
Founded on the west bank of the Mississippi in 1763
as a French trading post, the city grew rapidly in the
early 1800s as hundreds of pioneers poured in, hoping
to join wagon trains on their way west.

The city's population skyrocketed after steamboats began docking at St. Louis in 1817. Between 1815 and 1840, the number of residents in the city nearly tripled. Before long, St. Louis was the busiest, most important port on the upper Mississippi. Pioneers, traders, and adventurers all made their way through St. Louis to the new frontier. Further, farm supplies, food products, timber, and other goods all were shipped through St. Louis on their way east or west.

THE GREAT ST. LOUIS FIRE

On the evening of May 17, 1849, the steamboat White Cloud was tied up at the St. Louis docks. Suddenly, the steamboat caught fire. When its mooring lines burned, the *White Cloud* drifted downstream. Sparks from the blazing boat set fire to twenty-two other steamboats. Soon, wooden wharves and buildings along the waterfront caught fire, and the blaze quickly spread. By the time it was over, one-third of the city had been destroyed. Three people were killed in the Great St. Louis Fire.

Commerce and Travel

From the earliest days, the Mississippi River provided fur trappers, traders, farmers, and merchants with an excellent way to get their goods to market. The earliest trade along the river was in furs. Fur-trading posts dominated the upper Mississippi. Beaver was the fur of choice, but trappers also hunted deer, otter, mink, and even bear for skins.

As more people settled along the Mississippi, farming became an important part of the area's economy. The fertile lands along the river's banks were the perfect place for planting crops. Springtime floods replenished the soil's richness. The river itself was a good source of water for crops. Like fur trappers, farmers realized that the river was an excellent way to transport their goods to market.

Other early industries that sprang up along the river made the most of the Mississippi's awesome power. Some of the first mills on the Mississippi were constructed near St. Anthony's Falls. Sawmills were built to cut logs that were floated downriver from northern Minnesota and Wisconsin. Gristmills were constructed to grind grain.

Barges such as this one haul farm goods and other freight up and down the Mississippi River.

NATIVE NAMES

The five Midwest states that border the Mississippi River all have names with native roots.

Minnesota: "cloudy water"

Illinois (il-ih-NOY): from the name of the Illini people, meaning "men" or "warriors"

Iowa: "one who puts to sleep" or "beautiful land"

Missouri: "river of big canoes (kuh-NOOZ)"

Wisconsin: "gathering of the waters"

Traveling on the Mississippi

The first people to travel the Mississippi River were Native Americans using bark canoes (kuh-NOOZ). Early settlers modified the design of the canoes, making them larger in order to carry loads of fur and other trade items. As trade became an important part of the region's economy, the need for larger boats arose.

In the 1750s, river traders began using flatboats. Flatboats were bargelike craft that could be guided downriver from Minneapolis as far as New Orleans, Louisiana. Unfortunately, there was no way for the flatboats to get back up the river, so the big barges were chopped up and sold for timber. Flatboat crews had to make their way home by land.

Next came keelboats, large vessels propelled by long poles or hauled up the river by men pulling towropes along the riverbanks. Keelboats were much more effective than flatboats. They could be taken both down and up the river. During the days of the keelboats, a trip from Pittsburgh, Pennsylvania, to New Orleans might take only three weeks, while the return trip could take four months or more. In the 1810s, steamboats replaced keelboats as the preferred method of river travel.

This paddle-wheel ferry has been in operation since the Great Depression of the 1930s. Paddlewheelers have sailed the Mississippi since the early 1800s.

Steamboats Dominate the River

In 1811, the steamboat *New Orleans* became the first of its kind on the river. This event marked a new era in riverboat transportation. Soon, steamboats became the number-one way to transport goods up- and downstream. Steamboats were quicker and cheaper than flatboats and keelboats.

SHAKING THINGS UP

On December 16, 1811, the Mississippi River region was hit by the first of a series of powerful earthquakes. This earthquake, estimated to measure 8.0 or above on the Richter scale, was one of the most powerful in U.S. history. (The Richter scale measures the *magnitude*, or strength, of an earthquake.) The quake was so strong that it caused the Mississippi to flow in the opposite direction. The quake affected river cities from St. Louis to Memphis, Tennessee. One of the hardest-hit communities was New Madrid, Missouri. Town buildings there crumbled and fell into the river. The ground underneath New Madrid cracked and sank. Luckily, the earthquake caused few deaths: The area was not yet heavily populated. *Seismologists* (syze-MAHL-oh-jists), people who study earthquakes, say that the central Mississippi area suffers more earthquakes than any area in the United States east of the Rockies.

In the years following the voyage of the *New Orleans*, hundreds of steamboats began traveling up and down the Mississippi. The steamboats carried all types of human cargo: pioneers, trappers, traders, and soldiers. They also carried goods from port to port.

For steamboat captains, the river could be a dangerous place. Snags (hidden logs, rocks, and other debris), sandbars, shallow waters, and strong currents all took their toll on Mississippi steamboats. The stretch of the upper river between St. Louis, Missouri, and Cairo, Illinois was particularly dangerous. Steamboat pilots called this area "the Graveyard."

The steamboat era didn't last long. In the 1870s, railroads began competing with the ships. Soon, this faster, cheaper means of transportation put the steamboats out of business. Today, barges and diesel-powered towboats haul millions of tons of goods up and down the river.

Samuel Clemens (Mark Twain) became one of the most famous people in the world through his writing about life on the Mississippi River.

THE MAN FROM HANNIBAL

Samuel Langhorne Clemens grew up in Hannibal, Missouri, along the banks of the Mississippi River. Clemens loved the river and even spent four years working as a riverboat pilot. Later in life, Clemens immortalized the river in two famous books: *The Adventures of Tom Sawyer* and *The Adventures of Huckleberry Finn*. He wrote under the pen name "Mark Twain," which was a riverboat term. When the members of a riverboat crew called "mark twain," they were letting the pilot know that the water was deep enough for safe travel. Twain also wrote the nonfiction book *Life on the Mississippi*, which describes steamboating on the river.

Controlling the Mississippi

The Mississippi River has a history of deadly and damaging floods. In the springtime and during times of heavy rain, raging waters from the upper Mississippi, as well as the Ohio and Missouri Rivers, can wreak havoc on areas further downstream. Ever since people settled in the area, deadly floods have endangered homes, farms, livestock, and humans. During the worst floods, the river has risen as much as 50 feet (15 meters) above normal levels.

One of the first attempts to control flooding along the river was the creation of the Mississippi River Commission, established by Congress in 1879. The commission's goals were to improve river travel and control flooding. As a result, a channel 9 feet (2.7 meters) deep was dredged from Vicksburg, Mississippi, all the way north to Minneapolis. The deeper channel allowed bigger boats to travel all along the river. The commission also helped build levees along the river's banks. A levee is a high wall that is constructed to prevent a river from overflowing.

In April 1927, heavy rains caused the Mississippi to overflow its banks, flooding the homes of nearly 1 million people. The Great Mississippi Flood caused the deaths of as many as 1,000 people and ruined more than 5 million acres (2 million hectares) of farmland. It is considered one of the worst natural disasters in U.S. history.

After the 1927 flood, the U.S. government began looking for ways to prevent such a disaster from ever happening again. Beginning at Cairo, Illinois, the Army Corps of Engineers (en-jin-EERZ) began erecting high levees along the banks. At Cairo, the levees are 21 feet (6.3 meters) high. Floodways and spillways were also erected. These artificial (ar-tih-FISH-ul) channels divert floodwaters away from the river into other bodies of water, including artificial and natural lakes.

Although these improvements lessen the damage caused by flooding along the Mississippi, there is no way to prevent floods from occurring. Recent floods along the upper Mississippi took place in 1965, 1969, and 1973. In 1993, a flood caused serious damage to both the upper and lower Mississippi regions.

Today

Today, the Mississippi continues to be the most important inland waterway in the United States. Oil tankers and barges, as well as tourist boats, ply the waters, carrying everything from petroleum and lumber to wheat and rice. Because of its standing as an important trade area, the Mississippi region has attracted numerous industries over the year. Agriculture also continues to be a key part of the river economy.

As the Mississippi area becomes more crowded, increased pollution threatens the river. Sewage, fertilizer runoff, and chemicals (KEM-ik-ulz) from riverside factories are all causes of concern along the river today. Another serious problem is the decreasing amount of wetlands along the river. As wetlands disappear, native plants and animals are also in danger of disappearing. Spillways and levees, while important in reducing flood damage, have also reduced deposits of sediment that keep the wetlands healthy.

OXBOW LAKES

The upper Mississippi is famous for its many oxbow lakes. An *oxbow* lake is created on a U-shaped bend in the river. Over time, the river cuts back to its main course, creating a circular lake with a bit of land in the middle.

MORMONS ON THE MISSISSIPPI

In 1839, Joseph Smith, founder of the Church of Jesus Christ of Latter-day Saints, moved to the Mississippi. Smith and his followers, known as *Mormons*, were hoping to find a place where they would not be *persecuted*, or mistreated, because of their religion. Smith founded Nauvoo (nah-VOO), a town on the east bank of the Mississippi in Illinois. Over the next few years, 10,000 Mormons settled in Nauvoo, making it the biggest town in the state. Unfortunately, the Mississippi didn't prove to be the haven Smith had hoped for. In 1844, he and his brother Hyrum were jailed and then killed by an angry mob. Two years later, the Mormons abandoned the town. Thousands migrated to Salt Lake City in Utah.

Missouri
River

5

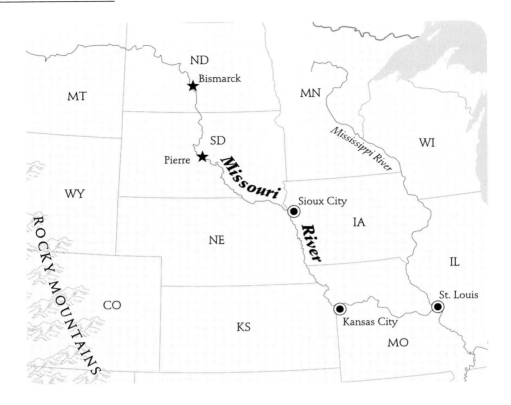

T he Missouri River is the longest river in the United States. The river has its source in southwestern Montana at Three Forks, the junction of the Gallatin, Jefferson, and Madison Rivers. The Missouri twists and stretches for more than 2,714 miles (4,342 kilometers), traveling south through the Dakota plains and four other Midwestern states. It ends its journey about 17 miles (27 kilometers) north of St. Louis, where it merges with the Mississippi River.

The Missouri River is the largest tributary of the Mississippi. Tributaries are smaller rivers and streams that flow into a bigger river. At one time, the Mississippi dumped as much as 800,000 cubic feet (22,400

WHAT'S IN A NAME?

The Missouri River was named for an area tribe, the Missouri people. The word may come from the Native American word meaning "river of big canoes (kuh-NOOZ)."

cubic meters) of water per second into the Mississippi. The Missouri drains an area of more than 529,000 square miles (1,375,400 square kilometers), which covers parts of ten U.S. states. Smaller rivers that flow into the Missouri include the Yellowstone, Cheyenne (shye-ANN), Platte, and Kansas Rivers.

The Missouri River has played a major role in the exploration and development of the West. Today it continues to be an important feature in the Midwest. Three state capitals are located on the Missouri: Jefferson City, Missouri; Bismarck, North Dakota; and Pierre, South Dakota. Other important riverfront cities include Kansas City, Missouri; Sioux (SOO) City, Iowa; and Omaha, Nebraska.

A fisherman tries his luck at the headwaters of the Missouri River near Three Forks, Montana.

GLACIERS AND THE MISSOURI RIVER

Thousands of years ago, before the last Ice Age, the Missouri River flowed north. It carried its waters from the Rocky Mountains to Hudson Bay. When glaciers advanced to the river from the north, they forced the Missouri to change course. Now the river flows south to the Mississippi instead. In addition, geologists say that the river today shows the approximate boundary of how far south Ice Age glaciers extended. To the northeast of the river, the huge beds of ice left behind glacial deposits. In these areas, soil is richer and softer. To the southwest, where glaciers didn't reach, the bedrock is harder and less fertile.

Settlement

The first people to settle near the Missouri River arrived about 15,000 years ago. Before the arrival of Europeans, Native American tribes used the river as a food source, fishing and growing crops in the fertile grounds on the river's banks. These tribes included the Crow, Omaha, Mandan, Hidatsa, Arikara, and Kansa. The native peoples were also the first to use the Missouri as a means of transportation. They built bark canoes (kuh-NOOZ) and dugouts from hollowed-out logs to journey up and down the river.

The first Europeans to see the mouth of the Missouri River were Frenchmen Jacques Marquette and Louis Jolliet in 1673. The two men, exploring the upper Mississippi, decided not to venture up the raging Missouri. In 1714, French explorer Étienne (AYT-yen) Venyard de Bourgmont explored the lower river. During his trip, he drew the first charts and maps of the area. The upper river was not explored until 1738, when French-Canadian Pierre Gaultier de Varennes (goht-YAY deh vuh-REN), sieur (lord) de la Vérendrye (vayr-ahn-DREE), explored the region. Vérendrye established a trading relationship with the local Mandan people.

In 1803, the United States bought a huge area of land in the west from France. The Louisiana Purchase, which doubled the size of the nation, included the area around the Missouri River. It allowed American exploration of a land that was wild, mysterious, and uncharted.

This painting shows the missionary explorers Jacques Marquette and Louis Jolliet as they travel with Native Americans in a canoe down the Mississippi River in 1672.

The Lewis and Clark Expedition

After the Louisiana Purchase, President Thomas Jefferson organized a team of adventurers to explore this new, unknown region. The team was led by Jefferson's private secretary, former army officer Meriwether Lewis, and his friend, William Clark. Jefferson hoped that his "Corps of Discovery" would find the Northwest Passage, a water route to the Pacific (puh-SIFF-ik) Ocean. The group was also charged with carefully mapping and describing the area.

On May 14, 1804, the forty-five men set out from a camp outside St. Louis, Missouri. Over the next six

Lewis and Clark, leaders of the expedition to explore the territory acquired by the Louisiana Purchase.

months, they followed the Missouri River, trading with the tribes they met along the way. In November, they built Fort Mandan in North Dakota and wintered there.

At Fort Mandan, the men met Sacagawea (sak-uh-juh-WEE-uh), a Shoshone (shoh-SHOH-nee) woman who was married to a French fur trapper. The Shoshone were a tribe of Native Americans who lived throughout the West. When Lewis and Clark continued their journey in the spring, Sacagawea went with them as a guide and interpreter. She played an important part in helping the expedition get across the Rocky Mountains.

The expedition followed the Missouri to the Rocky Mountains, which they crossed in August 1805. They were disappointed to find that there was no water route directly from the Rockies to the Pacific. Despite this setback, the group continued onward, and by November, they had achieved their goal: Lewis and Clark reached the Pacific Ocean in what is now Oregon.

After wintering in Oregon, the group began the return trip to St. Louis. They arrived there in September 1806. Although they had failed to find the Northwest Passage, Lewis and Clark provided the first accurate, extensive description of the new lands to the west. They also developed friendly relations with many Native American tribes along the way.

THE SPIRIT MOUND

On their journey to the Pacific (puh-SIFF-ik) Ocean, Lewis and Clark made a side trip to visit a large mound of dirt near Vermillion, South Dakota. The Native American tribes of the area believed that this mound was a place of evil. They called it "the hill of the little people," because they thought that tiny devils lived within the mound. In August 1804, Lewis and Clark set off to explore the fabled mound. They hiked 9 miles (14.4 kilometers) in the sweltering summer heat to the site. Then they climbed to the top of the 70-foot (21-meter) tall hill. Lewis and Clark determined that the hill was a natural formation. They saw no devils but many, many birds. Today, groups in South Dakota are working to restore Spirit Mound and the surrounding area to its 1804 condition.

The Overland Trails

After the Lewis and Clark expedition, people became interested in the new territory to the west. From members of the expedition, they heard stories of a land filled with beaver and other furry animals. They also learned that the Missouri was a good water route to the Rockies and that there were friendly native tribes along the way. Before long, groups of settlers began using the Missouri as a watery highway to the west.

Pioneers, such as those shown in this etching, headed west from St. Louis in the early 1800s and traveled along the Oregon and Santa Fe Trails.

Many of the pioneers who headed west on the overland trails began their journeys at cities near or along the Missouri. For example, many who traveled along the Oregon Trail set off from Independence (in-duh-PEN-dense), Missouri, just 3 miles (4.8 kilometers) from the big river. Other adventurers, on their way to New Mexico along the Santa Fe Trail, began their journey at a boat landing in Franklin, Missouri.

The cities along the Missouri thrived as thousands of pioneers flooded through them. City merchants supplied food, clothing, and other goods that would help the settlers reach their new homes. While many people only passed through the river towns, others stayed. Populations of the old towns boomed, while many new towns were settled along the river.

Controlling the Missouri River

In the early days of settlement along the Missouri, flooding was a problem. Each spring, rainwater and melting snow from the Rockies caused the river to overflow its banks. One of the worst early floods was the Great Flood of 1881. In the winter of that year, raging river waters caused serious damage in many river towns. A number of people were killed, animals and buildings were swept away, and whole towns were destroyed.

In 1944, the U.S. government decided that something must be done to control flooding along the Missouri. That year, Congress passed the Flood Control Act. The act established the Missouri River Basin Project, a program to construct dams along the big river.

In 1944, the first major dam on the river, Fort Peck Dam in Montana, was completed. Later, six more dams were constructed: Garrison, Oahe (oh-AH-hee), Big Bend, Fort Randall, Gavins Point, and Canyon Ferry. The dams control flooding on the Missouri by storing excess water from spring rain and melting snow. The extra water is then gradually released. Today, Missouri River dams make up the largest reservoir (REH-zerv-wahr) system in the United States.

The dams have improved water quality along the Missouri. The Missouri was once called "the Big Muddy," because of the amount of sediment in its waters. Today, it can no longer be called by its old nickname. The dams hold much of the sediment carried in the river waters. The dams and reservoirs are important sources of energy in the area. They provide electricity (ee-lek-TRISS-it-ee) to homes, farms, and businesses throughout the Missouri River region. The reservoirs also serve as recreation areas where people can enjoy fishing, boating, and swimming.

Despite the dams, flooding still occasionally occurs along the river. In 1993, for example, both the Missouri and Mississippi Rivers overflowed their banks from May through September. Thousands of homes were destroyed, bridges and roads were washed away, and fifty people were killed. The disaster, one of the worst in U.S. history, caused about $15 billion in damages.

Commerce

The Missouri River area is rich in natural resources. One of these resources was animal furs. Europeans used beaver, otter, mink, and fox fur to make hats, coats, and other items. As the supply of animals decreased in Europe, fur companies looked to the American Midwest as a new source.

> • *Fast Fact* •
> **The first permanent bridge to span the Missouri was the Hannibal and St. Joseph Railroad Bridge in Kansas City, Missouri. The bridge was completed in 1869.**

The first fur trappers and traders were the French, who traveled south from Canada in search of beaver and other pelts in the 1700s. These trappers used the Missouri as a pathway into the wilderness. They also traded with the native tribes that made their homes along the river. Early trappers used canoes to ply the river.

After the Louisiana Purchase, people began to found companies to exploit the animal wealth along the Missouri. One of the first to do so was Spaniard Manuel Lisa, who in 1809 founded the Missouri Fur Company with explorer William Clark and several other men. A competing company was the American Fur Company. Founded by German immigrant John Jacob Astor in 1808, the American Fur Company would eventually come to control the fur trade and make Astor one of the wealthiest men in the United States.

opposite:
The "Big Muddy" flows under the U.S. 92 Bridge in Leavenworth, Kansas.

The fur trade led to the development of the Missouri River region. Towns sprang up along the river to serve as fur-trading posts. The first permanent settlement in South Dakota, Fort Pierre, was started as a fur-trading post in 1817. Other well-known cities that got their start because of the fur trade include Kansas City, Missouri, founded in 1821 and St. Joseph, Missouri, established five years later.

THE MOUNTAIN MEN

From the early 1800s until the decline of the beaver in the 1840s, a special breed of man ruled the Missouri River wilderness—the mountain man. These fur trappers were tough, rugged, and solitary. For most of the year, the mountain men lived alone in the mountains. They braved dangerous animals, including grizzly bears, mountain lions, and rattlesnakes. They also fought off attacks from hostile Native Americans. In the winters, they had to somehow survive the freezing temperatures. Once a year, the trappers would come out of the wilderness and meet with merchants from St. Louis. Such a meeting was known as a *rendezvous* (RAHN-day-voo). At the rendezvous, trappers would sell their furs or exchange them for supplies from the East, such as new traps, guns, food, and liquor. In the early 1800s, more than 600 mountain men trapped furs near the Missouri. By the 1840s, with the number of beaver and other animals declining, the fur trade was nearly dead.

Steamboats Spark the Missouri Economy

Until the early 1800s, trappers, farmers, and other folk who wanted to send their goods to market had to use canoes, flat-bottomed keelboats, or mackinaw boats to travel the river. The mackinaw boat was built for a one-way trip downstream. At the end of its journey, it was taken apart, and the wood was sold or dumped.

Times changed in 1819, when the first steamboat cruised up the Missouri River. The steamboat *Independence* made a 200-mile (320-kilometer) trip from St. Louis to Franklin. Before long, goods were being shipped up and down the river by steamboat, and settlers and those heading west were also using the fast boats. Steamboats were the best way to get furs, grain, corn, and other goods down the river quickly. Tools, guns, traps, and other supplies traveled up the river.

The steamboat industry led to the rise of other businesses along the Missouri. Some of the businesses were directly related to steamboats. Steamboat docks, wood stations for fuel, and depots to connect passengers (PASS-en-jerz) to overland transportation all became important in the mid-1800s. Other businesses included saloons, hotels, and stores to serve the increasing traffic through port towns.

This photograph from 1878 shows the Rosebud, *an historic old Missouri River boat that went up the River from Bismark, North Dakota to Coalbanks, Montana.*

With the steamboats, however, came an increase in accidents and deaths on the Missouri. The river was difficult to navigate and dangerous in places. Pilots

were constantly on the lookout for snags, sandbars, and floating chunks of ice. During the nineteenth century (SEN-chur-ee), more than 400 steamboats got stuck and sank in the muddy Missouri waters.

In the 1870s, a new means of transportation arrived along the Missouri, and the days of the steamboat were numbered. By the early 1900s, railroads had put the steamboat industry out of business. Today, the river has once again become an important transportation route. Barges pushed by towboats move down the river, carrying grain, corn, and manufactured goods away from the Midwest to be sold around the world. They return loaded with fertilizer, cement, chemicals (KEM-ik-ulz), and other items.

Today

Each year, the American Rivers Organization lists rivers that face threats from such sources as pollution, overdevelopment, or damming. In 2001, the Missouri River was listed as the most endangered river in the United States. Some environmentalists estimate that one-third of the river has been altered by dams and channels built by people. Although the dams and reservoirs control flooding, they also disrupt the natural river ecosystem by destroying wildlife habitats. Experts say that some animal species (SPEE-sheez) may soon die out if water levels are not more carefully managed.

opposite:
A farm house is surrounded by water from the overflowing Missouri River.

In the past, pollution was another serious problem on the river. Fertilizers and pesticides (PESS-tih-sydez) from farm runoff, as well as sewage and industrial wastes, all made the river dirty and less healthy.

Although efforts to clean up the river have helped greatly, it may take years for the Missouri to recover.

The U.S. government has tried to protect parts of the Missouri River. It wants future generations (jen-er-AY-shunz) to experience (ex-PEER-ee-ense) the river the way it was when Lewis and Clark traveled on it. Today, two stretches of the river along the South Dakota-Nebraska border are part of the Missouri National Recreational River. The first stretch of river was set aside in 1978. In 1991, Congress agreed to protect a second stretch of river. In all, 57 miles (91 kilometers) of the river are protected.

Visitors to the Missouri National Recreation River can see the wild river as it once was. They may even see some endangered bird and fish species that make their homes here. They can also fish, boat, hike, and camp along the river. Winter activities include snowmobiling and cross-country skiing.

Ohio River

6

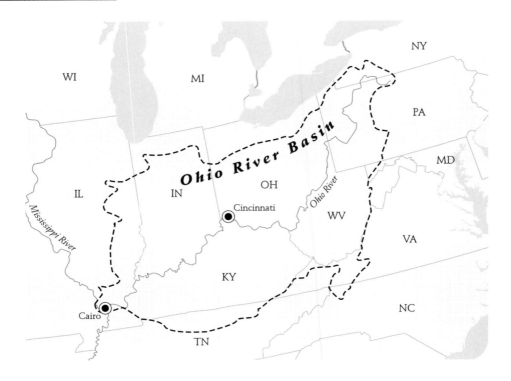

The Ohio River stretches 981 miles (1,570 kilometers) through three different regions of the United States. The river begins in the Northeast at Pittsburgh, Pennsylvania. It is formed by the joining of the Allegheny (al-uh-GAY-nee) and Monongahela (muh-non-guh-HEEL-uh) Rivers. The Ohio then flows southwest, winding its way through parts of the Midwest and the Southeast before joining the Mississippi River at Cairo, Illinois (il-ih-NOY). In the Midwest, the river forms the southern boundary for Ohio, Indiana, and Illinois.

The Ohio is a big river. It is the chief eastern tributary of the Mississippi River and supplies nearly half of the Mississippi's flow. (A tributary is a smaller river or stream that flows into a bigger river.) At its widest point, the Ohio is 1,600 feet (480 meters) wide. Its average depth is approximately 24 feet (7.2 meters). Major tributaries in the Midwest that flow into the Ohio include the Miami, Scioto (sye-OH-tuh), and Wabash Rivers.

The Ohio River has played an important role in our nation's history and growth. Because of its westward flowing direction, many settlers used the river as a highway to the west. The river also came to mark the boundary between the antislavery states in the North and the slaveholding states in the South. To slaves in Kentucky and other southern states, the river represented the final barrier to freedom.

WHAT'S IN A NAME?

The Ohio gets its name from an Algonquian (al-GAHN-kwee-an) word meaning "good river." The earliest French explorers called the river *La Belle Rivière*, or "the Beautiful River." The state of Ohio took its name from the river, which forms its southern boundary.

UNCLE TOM'S CABIN

In Harriet Beecher Stowe's controversial book *Uncle Tom's Cabin*, Stowe described a young slave mother trying to flee to freedom across the Ohio River. She based parts of her book on her own experiences (ex-PEER-ee-ense-ez): Having spent some time in Cincinnati (sin-sin-NAT-ee), Ohio, Stowe had witnessed the effects of slavery firsthand. On the other side of the river, in slave territory, Stowe had seen slave families being split up and sold away from one another. In this excerpt, Eliza attempts to escape the slave trader who has caught up with her.

It was now early spring, and the river was swollen and turbulent; great cakes of floating ice were swinging heavily to and fro in the turbid waters. . . .

The huge green fragment of ice on which she alighted pitched and creaked as her weight came on it, but she staid [*sic*] there not a moment. With wild cries and desperate energy she leaped to another and still another cake; stumbling-leaping-slipping-springing upwards again! Her shoes are gone—her stockings cut from her feet—while blood marked every step; but she saw nothing, felt nothing, till dimly, as in a dream, she saw the Ohio side, and a man helping her up the bank.

Boaters head down the Hocking River toward its junction with the Ohio River in Coolville, Ohio.

The Ohio River valley continues to be an important area of the nation. The river itself drains an area of more than 203,000 square miles (527,800 square kilometers). About 25 million people live in the valley, making it one of the most heavily populated areas in the country. Important Midwestern cities along the Ohio include Cincinnati (sin-sin-NAT-ee), Ohio; Jeffersonville and Evansville, Indiana; and Cairo, Illinois.

Settlement

The first people to make their homes in the Ohio River valley may have arrived 15,000 years ago. These early peoples hunted mammoths and mastodons (large, wooly creatures related to elephants), as well as other big animals that roamed the area. More than 2,000 years ago, the Adena and Hopewell Mound Builders lived along the river. Although these two groups disappeared before the arrival of European explorers, they left behind large dirt burial mounds along the riverbanks.

Later, other native tribes lived or hunted near the Ohio River. These tribes included the Shawnee, Miami, Omaha, Erie, and Susquehannock (suss-kweh-HANN-ok) people. Area tribes used the Ohio as a pathway for trade. They paddled canoes (kuh-NOOZ) between villages to visit and exchange goods.

The first Europeans to explore the Ohio were the French. René-Robert Cavelier (kav-ul-YAY), sieur (lord) de La Salle, may have explored the river as early as 1669. The French claimed control of the river. They recognized the importance of the waterway as a path between their holdings in Canada and Louisiana.

The British soon made it clear that they, too, wanted control of this important pathway to the West. The two nations began a struggle to control the Ohio River valley, as well as other areas of America, in the 1750s. The struggle escalated into the French and Indian War (1754–1763). When the war ended, Great Britain had emerged victorious. The British took control of the Ohio River the same year.

After winning control of the Ohio River valley, the British quickly issued a proclamation forbidding colonists to settle there. The British hoped to prevent conflict between the settlers and the native peoples who lived in the area. The proclamation was yet another source of hostility between the British and the American colonists. Soon the hostility would erupt into a full-blown war: the American Revolution (1775–1783).

After the revolution, the British handed over the Ohio River region to the United States. After George Rogers Clark's expedition on the river, people began coming into the area in droves. Many of them were veterans of the revolution who had received land grants instead of back pay. The population increased greatly after the 1820s.

GEORGE ROGERS CLARK

One American who left his mark on the Ohio River valley was George Rogers Clark. Clark was the older brother of explorer William Clark, who would make headlines as a leader of the Lewis and Clark expedition. An adventurer in his own right, George Rogers Clark was a leader of American troops during the American Revolution (1775–1783). Floating down the Ohio in 1778, Clark was responsible for taking control of many British settlements in what are now Indiana and Illinois (il-ih-NOY).

River Towns

As Americans began heading west in search of land, they quickly learned that the Ohio River was an important route. While many settlers used the river to move to new lands, others decided to settle along the river's fertile banks. As a result, many Ohio River towns were established. In fact, many of the earliest Illinois settlements were located along the river.

Marietta is the oldest permanent settlement along the Ohio River. Founded in 1788, the historic town also has the distinction of being the first permanent settlement in Ohio and the Northwest Territory. In 1788, Marietta was named the first capital of the Northwest Territory.

Also founded in 1788 was the settlement of Cincinnati, Ohio. The small town quickly became a center for trade, transportation, and culture in the Northwest Territory. In the mid-1800s, Cincinnati attracted immigrants from around the world, especially from Germany (JERM-an-ee), Eastern Europe, and Ireland. Shortly before the start of the Civil War (1861–1865), the city was the fourth-largest in the nation.

Another important city on the river's banks was Jeffersonville, Indiana. Laid out in 1802, the city was named after the man who had helped to design it: President Thomas Jefferson. From 1813 to 1816, Jeffersonville was the capital of the Indiana Territory.

NAMING CINCINNATI

Cincinnati, Ohio, was originally named Losantiville. *Losantiville* was a made-up word. It came from a combination of Latin, Greek, French, and Native American words that meant "the town opposite the mouth of the Licking River." Just two years after the town's founding, however, it was renamed for the Society (suh-SYE-uh-tee) of Cincinnati, a group created by officers of the American Revolution. The society was named for Cincinnatus, a statesman and patriot in ancient Rome.

Slavery and the Ohio River

Before the Civil War, the Ohio River was a key escape route for Southern slaves seeking freedom in the North. Some swam across this natural barrier. Others crossed in the wintertime, when huge chunks of ice floated on the river. Still others came to Ohio River cities by boat, relying on sympathetic captains to tell them where they might find a place of safety on the other side.

The Underground Railroad got its start along the northern banks of the Ohio River. Formed before the Civil War to guide runaway slaves to Canada and other safe areas, this group of caring individuals helped between 40,000 and 100,000 Southern blacks reach freedom. Cincinnati was one of the first stops for some of the slaves who fled on the Underground Railroad.

Many well-known abolitionists, people who wanted to end slavery, lived along the Ohio River. These are some of the most famous:

• *Levi Coffin*—Levi Coffin was a white Quaker who came to be known as "the president of the Underground Railroad." In 1847, Coffin moved to Cincinnati and opened a warehouse that sold goods made by free labor. Coffin and his wife Catherine personally helped hundreds of slaves escape to freedom.

• *John P. Parker*—This black abolitionist and businessman was one of the first conductors of the Underground Railroad. Parker, born into slavery in Virginia (ver-JINN-yuh), purchased his freedom at the age of eighteen. He later moved to Ripley, Ohio, where he helped many slaves cross the Ohio River from Kentucky.

• *Sojourner Truth*—Born Isabella Baumfree, Sojourner Truth was a slave in New York. After escaping in 1827, she changed her name and became a well-known abolitionist. Before the Civil War, Truth worked hard to convince people living on the northern banks of the Ohio River to shelter runaway slaves from the South.

In this 1898 illustration by artist Charles Webber, Levi Coffin, center background, and his wife, center foreground, are shown assisting slave escapees in Indiana. This illustration was used as a frontispiece for Wilbur Siebert's "The Underground Railroad from Slavery to Freedom."

Flooding and Flood Control

The Ohio River flows over its banks, flooding many towns along its course.

Over the years, the Ohio River has experienced (ex-PEER-ee-enst) severe floods. Springtime is the most common time for floods along the river. Disastrous floods in 1847, 1884, and 1913 wreaked havoc throughout the Ohio River valley.

The worst flood in the river's history occurred in 1937. That January, rain, snow, and sleet forced water levels up to a record-breaking height of 80 feet (24 meters). The flood devastated the city of Cincinnati and many other towns along the river. People watched helplessly as floodwaters carried away buildings, roadways, and livestock. Some towns were completely covered by the raging river. When the waters receded, about 190 people had been killed and damages exceeded $53 million.

After the 1937 flood, the federal government turned its attention to making the Ohio a safer river. Dams, channels, and locks were constructed to make the river safer from flooding disasters. The government also made it easier for boats to travel on the river by dredging in some places, making the river deeper.

A new lock and dam system was constructed along the Ohio in 1955. The new system had twenty locks and dams, replacing the old system of more than fifty locks and dams that had been completed in 1929. The new system stems flood damage, but nothing can completely control the big river. In 1997, flooding along the Ohio caused serious damage in the Midwest. About thirty people were killed, and floodwaters caused nearly $1 billion in damage.

Commerce and Travel

Even before Americans established settlements along the Ohio River, the river itself was an important avenue of transportation and trade. Native American tribes were the first to use the river as a path from one place to another. Later groups traveled through the Ohio River valley on their way from the East Coast to the lands in the West.

Not surprisingly, one of the first industries to spring up along the river was boatbuilding. Flatboat builders made a living by ferrying settlers down the Ohio from the East. At the end of the route, the flatboats were torn apart and used for building material or firewood. The keelboat was another type of boat that ferried people and goods down the river. Unlike flatboats, keelboats could make the trip both up and down the river. Both keelboats and flatboats also served as floating stores, churches, and even bordellos. The boats would move from town to town, bringing their services with them.

The Coming
of the Steamboat

The invention of the steam engine brought a new era to the Ohio River. One of the first steamboats to make regular runs on a river was the *New Orleans*,

The Mississippi Queen *heads down the Ohio River, passing under the Maysville Suspension Bridge.*

built on the Ohio. In October 1811, the *New Orleans* began its first trip on the river. It took two weeks for the boat to reach the mouth of the Mississippi at New Orleans, Louisiana.

Steamboats were a boon to trade along the Ohio. Goods and passengers could be transported more quickly—and more cheaply—than ever before. In the 1820s, a number of canals were constructed to further improve trade along the river. In just two decades, seven canals were dug. One important canal was the Ohio and Erie Canal. Along with the Miami and Erie Canal, this canal connected the Ohio River with the Great Lakes.

In the 1850s, steamboats faced their first competition for trade along the river: railroads. At first, the steamboats and trains operated hand in hand. Packets, which were small steamers, ran between Cincinnati and Pittsburgh, the last stop on the Pennsylvania Railroad. In 1868, however, the first railroad bridge crossing the Ohio was built. Before long, neither the steamers nor the canals were as important as they had once been.

Despite the railroads, the Ohio River has continued to be an important shipbuilding and boatbuilding location. During World War II (1939–1945), many wartime vessels were built in shipyards along the river. Today, some Ohio River towns continue to operate shipyards.

Today

The Ohio River is still an important trade route. Each year, more than 230 million tons (207 million metric tons) of goods are shipped along the river. About 70 percent of all the freight shipped up and down the river is energy-producing products, such as coal and petroleum. Other goods include items manufactured in plants along the river, such as appliances (uh-PLYE-an-sez), pharmaceuticals (far-

muh-SOO-tik-ulz), and automobiles. These goods are carried up and down the river by big barges.

The Ohio River valley is also a beautiful, scenic area. The river itself is dotted with small islands, and tall cliffs rise on both sides. Since the 1800s, however, the river's beauty has been threatened. As the number of factories, farms, and houses along the river increased, so did the pollution. Industrial waste, discharges from slaughterhouses (SLAW-ter-how-sez), and raw sewage from riverfront cities all damaged the Ohio, making it an unsafe place to fish or swim.

In the mid-1900s, environmentalists and other people who cared about the Ohio River began looking for ways to clean it. In 1948, the Ohio River

A barge is moved into place to offload gasoline from another barge at the bottom of the photo. The lower barge ruptured and spilled thousands of gallons of fuel into the Ohio River.

Valley Sanitation Commission (ORSANCO) was established. Over the years, ORSANCO has helped get laws passed to control pollution going into the river. As a result, any waste from riverside factories must be treated before it can go into the river. In 1995, all wastewater from Ohio River cities was treated twice before it was released back into the river. Companies that break the laws and pollute the Ohio can be fined. Today, the river is once more the home to many different species (SPEE-sheez) of fish. In fact, a number of fishing tournaments are held on the river each year. People can even swim in the river again.

opposite:
Boaters speed
along the smooth
waters of the
Ohio River.

OHIO RIVER HISTORY MAKERS

William Howard Taft, the twenty-seventh president of the United States, was born in Cincinnati, Ohio, in 1857. After serving as president from 1909 to 1913, Taft was selected to become chief justice of the United States Supreme Court. He is the only president to be so honored.

Edwin M. Stanton, the secretary of war under President Abraham Lincoln, was born in Steubenville, Ohio, in 1814.

Ulysses (yoo-LISS-eez) *S. Grant* was born in 1822 in Point Pleasant, Ohio. He later served as the commander-in-chief of the Union army during the Civil War. In 1868, Grant was elected the eighteenth U.S. president.

William Henry Harrison, the ninth U.S. president, is buried in North Bend, Ohio, overlooking the Ohio River. Harrison died after just one month in office. His grandson Benjamin was born in North Bend. Benjamin became the twenty-third U.S. president.

Adolph Simon Ochs—Adolph Ochs, an important newspaper publisher, was born in Cincinnati, Ohio, in 1858. Ochs was just twenty years old when he founded the *Chattanooga Times* in 1878. Nineteen years later, he purchased a struggling paper called the *New York Times*. Ochs built the *Times* into one of the most respected newspapers in the world. He adopted the paper's famous slogan: "All the News That's Fit to Print."

The Ohio River has once again become a popular attraction for visitors and area residents. People can tour the river in nineteenth-century style, on paddlewheel riverboats. They can also sail or speedboat along the river. Area attractions include the Cincinnati Zoo, the birthplace of President William Howard Taft, and Angel Mounds State Historic Site. Angel Mounds contains a re-creation of a Mound Builders' village.

• *Fast Fact* •

Cairo, Illinois is located at the point where the Ohio River and the Mississippi River meet. The town was named for Cairo, Egypt (EE-jipt).

Ozark Mountains

7

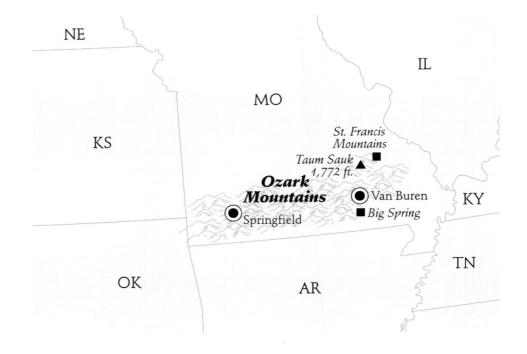

The Ozark Mountains are a region of high hills and deep valleys that stretch more than 50,000 square miles (130,000 square kilometers) east to west. They begin in southern Illinois (il-ih-NOY) and continue through the southern half of Missouri in the Midwest. Also called the Ozark Plateau or the Ozarks, the hills continue into northern Arkansas (AR-ken-saw) and eastern Oklahoma. Most of the Ozarks—33,000 square miles (85,800 square kilometers)—are located in Missouri.

The Ozarks are made up of a number of different mountain chains. The highest peaks are found in the Southeast, in the Boston Mountains of Arkansas. In the Midwest, the highest peak is Taum Sauk Mountain in Missouri's St. Francis (fran-SWAH) Mountains. Taum Sauk, which rises to a height of more than 1,770 feet (531 meters), is Missouri's tallest mountain.

The Ozark region is home to hundreds of springs, caves, sinkholes, and rivers. The entire area is bordered by the Missouri River to the north and the Mississippi River to the east. The Black, Osage, Current, and Gasconade Rivers drain the Midwest Ozarks.

> • *Fast Fact* •
> A *sinkhole* **is a cave whose roof has collapsed, leaving a large, bowl-shaped depression in the ground.**

Settlement

The first humans to make their homes in the Ozark area arrived about 12,000 years ago. These early people were the ancestors (AN-sess-terz) of later groups of Native Americans. Three thousand years ago, people known as the Bluff Dwellers settled in caves near the White River in the Ozarks. The Bluff Dwellers hunted in the area and were the first group to grow crops there.

COMPARING THE OZARKS

Although the Ozarks are called mountains, they are actually a series of hills cut out of a former plateau by wind and water erosion. Here's how the Ozarks' highest peak compares to those of other mountain ranges.

Mountain System	Name of Highest Peak	Height of Highest Peak
Ozarks	Taum Sauk	1,772 feet (532 meters)
Adirondacks	Mount Marcy	5,344 feet (1,603 meters)
Appalachians	Mount Mitchell	6,684 feet (2,005 meters)
Black Hills	Harney Peak	7,242 feet (2,173 meters)
Rockies	Mount Elbert	14,433 feet (4,330 meters)

Before the first Europeans arrived, several tribes of Native Americans lived near the Ozarks. The most powerful group was the Osage, who were known as a fierce, warlike people. They used the hilly Ozark area as their hunting grounds. Many of the trails and roads that now cut through the Ozarks were initially hunting trails forged by the Osage.

In the early 1800s, other groups of Native Americans began settling in the Ozark area. Many were tribes that had been forced off their lands in the Northeast by early American settlers. The groups who moved to the Ozarks included the Kickapoo, Delaware, Shawnee, and Cherokee.

Europeans and Americans in the Ozarks

The first nonnative people to explore the Ozark region were French trappers who began exploring the area in the early 1700s. The French traded with the Osage. They bartered weapons and trinkets for beaver and buffalo skins.

The French were also the first to realize that the Ozarks were filled with natural riches. They began mining the Ozark hills for lead, founding small settlements near the mines. One of these early settlements was Potosi, founded in 1763 as a French mining camp called Mine au Breton.

In 1803, the Ozarks became part of the United States as part of the Louisiana Purchase. Two years later, American explorer Zebulon Pike traveled near the hills, but did not enter the Ozark area. The first American to carefully explore the region was Henry Rowe Schoolcraft. In the winter of 1818, Schoolcraft, an American explorer and geologist, spent three months in the Ozarks. He kept careful notes on his expedition, describing the hills, rivers, caves, minerals, plants, and animals he saw. During his trip,

Schoolcraft met several mountain men who eked out a living trapping in the area. The adventurer also met some of the Osage people.

This postcard image shows a bustling College Street in Springfield, Missouri early in the twentieth century.

Schoolcraft's description of the Ozarks encouraged people from the Southeast to migrate to the area. Beginning in the 1820s, hundreds of American settlers from Kentucky, Tennessee, the Carolinas, and Virginia (ver-JINN-yuh) settled in the region. Many of the early hill pioneers were of Scotch-Irish descent. They made their homes around the many springs of the area. The springs provided water for drinking and farming, as well as power for gristmills and sawmills.

Although people continued to migrate into the Ozarks, the area had few large cities. The largest, Springfield, Missouri, became important because it was located near westward migration routes. Settled in 1829, Springfield became the largest city in the Ozarks. In 2000, 151,000 people lived there.

HENRY ROWE SCHOOLCRAFT

Henry Rowe Schoolcraft spent his life visiting and writing about unexplored land throughout the United States. Born in upstate New York in 1793, Schoolcraft studied geology and mineralogy in college. After graduating, the young man headed west to explore the frontier wilderness. During his trips, he kept careful and colorful notes. Two years after his 1818 trip through the Ozarks, Schoolcraft took part in another important expedition, exploring the upper Mississippi Valley and Lake Superior. During his travels, the explorer became very interested in Native American languages and culture. He wrote more than thirty books on these topics. Henry Wadsworth Longfellow later used Schoolcraft's books as references when he wrote his famous poem *Hiawatha*. Schoolcraft died in 1864.

Because of its hilly, rugged terrain, the Ozark region was the last part of Missouri to be settled. By 1835, however, new arrivals were beginning to displace many of the native people from the land. Most of the tribes were forced to Indian Territory in Kansas and Oklahoma.

Migration into the area was disrupted by the Civil War (1861–1865). Once the war had ended, large groups of immigrants made their way to the Ozarks. These groups included German, Swedish, Polish, Italian, and Hungarian people. In recent years, the region has seen an influx of Hispanic and Vietnamese immigrants.

The Civil War

In 1818, the United States was made up of twenty-two states: eleven slaveholding states and eleven free states. That year, Missouri requested statehood. As a slaveholding state, Missouri would have upset the balance between free and slave states. Over the next

Dred Scott, a slave who took up residence in a territory where slavery had been banned by the Missouri Compromise, sued for his freedom in 1848. The Supreme Court ruled that Scott must remain a slave.

three years, the U.S. Congress worked on a compromise (KOMM-proh-myze) to maintain this delicate political balance.

In 1820, the Missouri Compromise was enacted by Congress. As a result of the compromise, Maine was admitted to the Union as the twenty-third state— a free state. The following year, slaveholding Missouri became the twenty-fourth U.S. state. In addition, slavery was abolished in the Louisiana Territory north of the boundary between Arkansas and Missouri. The compromise would last until 1854.

In 1861, the Civil War split families and neighbors throughout Missouri. In this border state between the

opposite:
Arch Clements,
Dave Pool, and
Bill Hendricks
brandish their
guns. The three
men were part of
a group of
Confederate Army
outlaws called
Quantrill's
Raiders.

North and the South, the war caused conflict and controversy. Although Missouri never seceded from the Union, many people within the state sided with the Confederacy.

Hundreds of Civil War skirmishes took place in the Ozarks. Most of these battles were guerrilla warfare: ambushes and surprise raids by bands of antislavery "jayhawkers" and proslavery "bushwhackers." With its hills, caves, and hiding places, the Ozark region was the perfect place for this type of warfare.

One band of guerrillas who hid out in the Ozarks was Quantrill's Raiders. Led by Confederate William Clarke "Guerrilla" Quantrill, the raiders included as many as 300 men. Some of them, such as Frank and Jesse James, and Cole Younger of the notorious James Younger Gang, later became infamous outlaws of the Wild West.

The slightest mention of Quantrill's name was enough to strike fear into the hearts of people living in pro-Union towns in Missouri and Kansas. Quantrill and his band raided towns and farming areas, taking food, weapons, and other supplies. They were quite willing to kill in the name of the Confederacy. In 1863, Quantrill and his men murdered more than 180 men and boys in Lawrence, Kansas. The outlaw was killed two years later in Kentucky by Union troops. He was just twenty-seven years old.

ALF BOLIN, BAD BUSHWHACKER

Of all the Civil War guerrillas in the Ozarks, the worst by far was Alfred "Alf" Bolin. Bolin, leading a group of about twenty men, committed robbery, murder, and mayhem throughout the Ozark region. Although he claimed to sympathize with the South, Bolin killed both Union and Confederate supporters. Bolin bragged that he had killed as many as forty people, ranging in ages from twelve to eighty years old. His life of crime ended when he was killed by a Union soldier. The outlaw's head was carried to the town of Ozark, Missouri, where it was displayed in the town square on a pole. People came from miles around to have one last look at the bad bushwhacker.

One of Missouri's most important Civil War battles took place in the Ozarks. The Battle of Wilson Creek was fought in August 1861, outside of Springfield. The battle was bloody, causing heavy damage on both sides. Nearly one out of every four Union soldiers on the battlefield was killed, including Union general (JEN-er-ul) Nathaniel Lyon. Although Confederate troops took control of Springfield, they only held onto it for six months before the Union took it back.

Henry Clay, American statesman, was a major promoter of the Missouri Compromise of 1820.

Mountain Dangers

The Ozarks are home to some extreme weather. Tornadoes, heavy winds, and raging thunderstorms are all common. Most Ozark tornadoes occur in April and May, although the most dangerous ones often occur in early autumn. In April 1880, a tornado destroyed the small town of Marshfield, Missouri, killing about sixty-five people. Over the years, advanced weather technology (tek-NAHL-oh-jee) and early warning systems have lessened the number of deaths. Since 1990, only two Missouri residents have died because of tornadoes.

A shed is inundated by the floodwater from the Osage River in the Ozark mountains of Missouri.

Near Ozark rivers, flooding can be a problem. Over the years, flash floods have caused deaths and destruction. A flash flood is a sudden flood caused by very heavy rainfall. Within a matter of minutes, rivers can rise as much as 30 feet (9 meters), washing away buildings, people, and trees. In recent years, dams have been built along Ozark rivers to control flooding.

MARVEL CAVE

The Missouri Ozarks are home to thousands of caves. Marvel Cave, located in Silver Dollar City, is one of the most famous in the region. First discovered by the Osage people, the cave was later explored by Henry T. Blow in 1869. At one time, the cave was used as a source of bat droppings—called *guano*—which were used as fertilizer. In 1894, Marvel Cave was opened to the public for visits. Since then, thousands of people have visited the deepest cave in Missouri, admiring such unique (yoo-NEEK) attractions as the 210-foot (63-meter) high Cathedral Room and 32 miles (51 kilometers) of explored passageways.

Too little water can also be a problem in the Ozarks. Summer droughts (DROWTZ), common in the region, can kill crops and livestock and also cause forest fires.

Commerce

Even before Europeans arrived, native people farmed the fertile soil of the Ozark valleys. They grew corns, beans, and squash. Later, settlers grew other crops, including tomatoes, strawberries, apples, grapes, wheat, and peaches. Beef, poultry, and dairy farms are still important in the Ozark region.

During the days of early American settlement, another important part of the Ozark area economy was the timber industry. Beginning in the early 1800s, timber companies razed huge areas of Ozark forestland. Trees were sent to area sawmills and turned into planks and boards used to build up the Midwest and West.

opposite: Visitors to Onondaga Cave in Leasburg, Missouri wind their way along a secure path. Water and other elements have created a variety of formations inside the cave.

In the 1870s, the lumber was used to make railroad ties. Timber from the Ozarks was used for thousands of miles of track throughout the nation. People who cut the trees for railroad ties became known as tie whackers. The heavy lumbering in the late 1800s and early 1900s wiped out the old-growth forests in the Ozarks, destroying ecosystems and causing the disappearance of some types of area wildlife. Bears, mountain lions, and otters all suffered as their habitats were destroyed.

Mining the Ozark Hills

Another important area industry was mining. Lead was discovered in the Ozark hills in the early 1700s, and the area quickly became known as the Lead Belt. One of the most successful mining companies was the St. Joseph Lead Company. The company, founded in 1864, started a mining boom in the area. Before long, hundreds of people were busy mining the Ozark hills. Missouri towns like Iron Mountain, Pilot Knob, Webb City, and Oronogo got their start because of nearby mining companies. Mining was also an important part of the economies of Springfield and Joplin, Missouri.

Lead wasn't the only valuable mineral in the Ozarks. Miners also took zinc, barite, and copper from the hills. Today, mining continues to be an important industry in the area. Missouri produces 60 percent of the U.S. lead supply. Natural gas, limestone, and granite also come from the Ozarks.

Today

In the Ozarks today, tourism is the most important industry. The region is home to many natural attractions, including its numerous springs. The largest of the springs is Big Spring near Van Buren,

Missouri. Each day, more than 200 million gallons (760 million liters) of water flow from Big Spring into the nearby Current River. Other springs include Greer Spring, Blue Spring, and Boiling Spring.

Dams constructed on Ozark rivers for flood-control purposes also provide summer fun. Two big bodies of water, the Lake of the Ozarks and Taneycomo Lake, are well known for swimming, fishing, and boating. In addition, Mark Twain National Forest in Missouri includes more than 100,000 acres (40,000 hectares) for visitors to enjoy. Established in 1933, the park includes many areas where trees have been replanted to undo years of damage caused by the lumber industry.

In 1959, the small town of Branson, Missouri, turned to tourism to boost its fortunes. Since that time, Branson has become known as one of the country music capitals of the world. Each year, millions of people flock to the city to shop, see shows, and listen to live country music. It has become one of the top tourist destinations in the nation.

Country singer Boxcar Willie poses in front of his country music theater in Branson, Missouri.

Pollution Problems

As more people discover the natural beauty of the Ozarks, pollution problems grow. Water pollution is a serious concern in some parts of the Ozark region. In such areas, people are forced to boil their water before drinking it. The pollution affects swimming and other summer water sports. It also affects wildlife in the region. Fish that swim in Ozark lakes and rivers have been found to have high levels of pollutants in their bodies.

Keeping rivers and lakes clean and healthy has become a priority for area residents. The Watershed Committee of the Ozarks asks people to practice water conservation and preservation at home. It also organizes groups to check the quality of area rivers and lakes.

Another group, Missouri Stream Teams, has people adopt local streams. Among other things, Stream Teams keeps their waterways free of litter and checks for pollution. Over the years, thousands of people have worked on Stream Teams to make sure that Missouri water stays clean and healthy.

Red River
of the North

8

opposite:
The Red River
winds through
farmland in
western
Minnesota.

The Red River of the North is a 545-mile-long (872-kilometer-long) river that twists its way through part of the Midwest. The river is formed where the Bois de Sioux (bwah deh SOO) and Otter Tail Rivers meet in western Minnesota. From there, the narrow, shallow river flows north, forming the boundary between North Dakota and Minnesota. It stretches into southern Canada, where it empties into Lake Winnipeg in Manitoba.

The history of the Red River of the North begins more than 2 million years ago, when glaciers covered the area. The weight and movement of these glaciers compressed and scraped the earth, leaving the land below flat and level. As global temperatures rose, the huge blocks of ice retreated to the north. They left behind a glacial lake called Lake Agassiz (AGG-uh-see). At its largest, Lake Agassiz may have stretched more than 700 miles (1,120 kilometers) in length and covered more than 100,000 square miles (260,000 square kilometers). More than 9,000 years ago, the lake's waters receded. Left behind was the flat, fertile lake bed. The Red River flows through the center of the old bed.

Today, the Red River and its surrounding valley make up an important agricultural area. The soil near the river is rich and fertile, and the river itself provides water for crops and livestock. Tributaries of the Red River include the Red Lake and Sheyenne (shye-ANN) Rivers.

Settlement

Thousands of years ago, the land near the Red River was covered with prairie grasses. The grasses attracted buffalo, deer, and other wild animals to feed. For early Native American tribes, the Red River valley was an excellent hunting ground. Such tribes as the Sioux (SOO), Metis, Cheyenne (shye-ANN), Mandan, and Ojibwa (oh-JIB-wah) all took advantage of the plentiful game that could be found along the Red River.

The first Europeans to explore the Red River area were the French. In the 1730s, Pierre Gaultier de Varennes (goht-YAY deh vuh-REN), sieur (lord) de la Vérendrye (vayr-ahn-DREE), explored the river. The French claimed the area, but the English also were interested. Both groups realized the river's potential (poh-TEN-chul) as a source for animal furs. Both the French and the English quickly established trading posts along the river.

WINNIPEG, CANADA

The Red River played an important role in U.S. history. The river was also important to the settlement of Canada. The first settlement on the Red River was in Winnipeg, located in Manitoba, Canada. In 1738, French explorer Pierre Gaultier de Varennes (goht-YAY deh vuh-REN), sieur (lord) de la Vérendrye (vayr-ahn-DREE), built a trading post at the river's mouth. He named the trading post Fort Rouge (Fort Red). The town of Winnipeg was permanently settled in 1812 by Lord Selkirk, a Scottish nobleman. Selkirk bought the area from the Hudson's Bay Company and settled a group of Scottish homesteaders there. The town became known as the Red River Settlement; its inhabitants were called Selkirkers. In 1870, Winnipeg was named the capital of Manitoba.

To obtain the animal furs, the French and English traders established relationships with the Native American tribes in the area. The traders exchanged tools, trinkets, and alcohol for valuable animal pelts to ship back East. Animals valued for their skins included buffalo, deer, beaver, fox, and mink.

The first trading posts on the Red River were built along the upper portion of the river, in the area that is now Canada. One of the earliest trading posts erected along the lower Red River was built in 1797. That year, the Northwest Company constructed a fur post at present-day Pembina, North Dakota. Pembina became the first permanent settlement in North Dakota when a group of Scottish farmers called the Selkirkers made their homes there.

Another early settlement in the Red River area was Grand Forks, North Dakota. Grand Forks got its start as a fur-trading post in 1801. The site was named by French fur traders for its location at the junction of the Red and Red Lake Rivers. Permanent settlement of the site would not occur until 1869.

One of the dangers of settlement along the Red River is the possibility of annual flooding. This 1997 photograph shows downtown Grand Forks, North Dakota covered in water when the Red River rose to more than twenty-five feet above flood level.

The Dakota Boom

In the 1860s, more and more people began to settle in Minnesota east of the Red River. Problems arose between the native tribes in the area and the settlers. The new arrivals wanted the best lands for themselves. Slowly, the Sioux and other tribes were pushed further and further west.

In August 1862, the Sioux began to fight back. The conflict, known as the Sioux Uprising, began in Minnesota. Led by Little Crow, the Sioux attacked and killed hundreds of settlers.

The Sioux Uprising quickly spread to the Red River area. In late August, Breckenridge (BREHK-en-rihj), Minnesota, at the headwaters of the river, was attacked and destroyed by the Sioux warriors. Eventually, U.S. troops squelched the rebellion, and the remaining Sioux people were forced onto reservations, or lands set aside for them, in the Badlands of South Dakota.

Badlands National Park, located in southwestern South Dakota, is made up of 244,000 acres of eroded buttes, spires, and pinnacles, and the largest, protected mixed grass prairie in the United States.

With the native peoples out of the way, the U.S. government granted the Northern Pacific (puh-SIFF-ik) Railroad millions of acres of land in the west. Much of this land was in North Dakota. The government wanted to attract settlers and homesteaders to the western lands and knew that railroad access into the area would do just that.

To finance its new railway, the Northern Pacific began selling off chunks of land to people willing to settle in the area. Adventurous people jumped at the opportunity, buying up thousands of acres for farming. This marked the beginning of the Dakota Boom, as a rush of homesteaders flooded into North Dakota to work the land.

One important Midwestern city that had its roots in the Dakota Boom was Fargo, North Dakota. Established by the Northern Pacific Railroad in 1871, the town was first called Centralia. The railway crossed the Red River from Moorhead, Minnesota to Centralia. The town's name was later changed to honor William George Fargo, one of the founders of Wells Fargo & Company, a mail delivery service. Fargo was also a director of the Northern Pacific.

THE WICKEDEST CITY IN THE WORLD

In 1871, Moorhead, Minnesota was settled across the Red River from Fargo, North Dakota. Moorhead, which started off as a camp for railroad workers, quickly earned a nasty reputation for itself. However, its reputation as "the Wickedest City in the World" didn't take firm hold until 1889. That year, North Dakota was admitted to the Union as a "dry" state. This meant that alcohol was strictly forbidden throughout the state. Soon, residents from Fargo were crossing the river to Moorhead to have a drink. Moorhead's saloons and dance halls stayed open seven days a week, and gambling and violent behavior were common. Moorhead remained the "sin city" of the Midwest until 1915. That year, Clay County, Moorhead's home, became a dry county and liquor was banned.

Flooding on the Red River

The Red River is sometimes called "the American Nile." Like the Nile in Egypt (EE-jipt), the Red River is the site of nearly annual flooding. Because the Red River valley is so flat, floods can spread for miles and last for weeks before waters drain away.

Some of the worst floods along the Red River have taken place in the spring. Melting snow and spring rains can cause serious damage to river towns

Floodwaters from the Red and Wild Rice Rivers take over the Forest River area of Fargo, North Dakota.

and surrounding areas. However, summer floods are also common.

Over the years, floods along the Red River have taken lives, destroyed crops, and damaged roads, buildings, and bridges. One of the first recorded floods along the river occurred in 1826. That year, floodwaters drove many early settlers off their lands forever.

During the twentieth century (SEN-chur-ee), people living along the Red River looked for ways to stem flood damage. Drainage ditches, earthen dikes, and dams have all helped contain the river waters during flood season. Despite the many improvements, it is impossible to completely prevent Red River flooding.

One of the worst floods ever to occur along the river was in spring 1997. The previous winter, numerous snowstorms left heavy snow on the ground. In April, when rain and warm temperatures quickly melted the snow, the river overflowed its banks. In just days, the flooding had set records. At Fargo, waters crested at 54 feet (16.2 meters). More than ten people were killed by the floodwaters, and area towns suffered more than $4 billion in damages.

Commerce and Travel

One of the first industries along the Red River was the fur trade. In the early 1800s, buffalo, beaver, and other skins were sent from fur-trading posts at Pembina and other Red River sites to St. Paul, Minnesota. However, the Red River was a very crooked, twisting river. To travel from one point to another along the river often took twice as long as the same trip on land.

Early Red River traders shipped their goods by land, not water. The furs and other goods were loaded onto carts that were hauled overland by teams of oxen. (Oxen are large farm animals related to cows.) It could take up to two months for these "Red River oxcarts" to complete the trip between Pembina and St. Paul.

Boats and Trains

For many years, the sight of trains of Red River oxcarts along the river was common. Because this method of transportation was so slow, however, businesspeople in St. Paul began looking for a way to move goods up and down the Red River in a more timely fashion. In 1858, the St. Paul Chamber of Commerce offered $2,000 to anyone who could put a steamboat into operation on the Red River.

Anson Northup, a businessman from St. Paul, took the chamber up on its offer. Northup purchased a boat called the *North Star*, which had been sailing the Mississippi, a much bigger, deeper river. Northup altered the design of the boat so that it would operate effectively on the shallow Red River. In the spring of 1859, the boat, now named the *Anson Northup*, went into operation. Northup got his money from the chamber of commerce.

The *Anson Northup* didn't last long on the Red River. Just one year after it began cruising up and down the river, the boat sank. In 1862, a bigger steamboat called the *International* began operating on the river. This boat was 136 feet (41 meters) long and could carry 172 tons (155 metric tons). Like the other steamers that would ply the Red River, the *International* often found itself sitting at the docks during the late summer. At this time of year, the Red River was too shallow to use big steamboats.

The early 1870s were the glory days of steamboating along the Red River. In 1872, the Red River Transportation Line went into business. By 1874, five steamboats were working the river, competing for the chance to carry goods and passengers (PASS-en-jerz).

The steamboat was important to river trade for only a very short time. The Northern Pacific Railroad arrived in North Dakota in 1871 and crossed the Red River by 1872. By 1878, the railroad had put the steamboats out of business. Trains were cheaper, quicker, and less dangerous than the big boats.

The Bonanza Farms

The historic Mankato Holstein Farm Barn was the largest barn in Minnesota when it was built in 1919.

As the fur trade dwindled in the mid-1800s, another business took its place: agriculture. Settlers quickly discovered that the soil along the Red River was rich and fertile. The word spread, and the area soon became known as one of the best farming areas in the United States.

With huge chunks of fertile farmland available for the taking, some businesspeople realized that they could make money in the Red River area. Beginning in the 1870s, a number of them bought up thousands of acres of land for wheat farming. Instead of working the farms themselves, these absentee landowners hired managers (MAN-uh-jerz) to run the farms for them. Called bonanza farms, because they were a sure source of money, the operations required hundreds of workers and a lot of equipment to keep them running.

The first bonanza farm was created in 1875. That year, Oliver Dalrymple (dal-RIM-pul) managed a farm of more than 40,000 acres (16,000 hectares) for

the Northern Pacific Railroad. Dalrymple's success and a demand for Dakota wheat led to the establishment of many other bonanza farms in the Red River valley. During the heyday of these giant "factory farms," there were more than ninety in operation. One bonanza farm operation even owned its own steamboat line to ship its wheat to other parts of the country.

The era of the bonanza farms ended in the 1920s, but farming is still the most important industry in the Red River area. Today, wheat, sugar beets, soybeans, sunflowers, potatoes, barley, and corn are all produced in the Red River valley. Each summer, migrant workers from Mexico and other areas pour into North Dakota and Minnesota to work the fields during harvest time.

opposite:
A modern-day farmer checks the condition of his corn in a field in the Red River valley.

Today

Today, there is little industrial traffic along the Red River. The boats that ply the river waters are mostly tourist and recreational boats. The Red River is known for its catfish fishing, and people come from miles around to fish here.

In recent years, the river has been affected by pollution from nearby farms and cities. Because many people who live in the area depend upon the Red River for their water, it is important that the river be kept clean. Groups such as River Keepers, an environmental organization based in the Fargo-Moorhead area, work to make sure that the river remains healthy.

Sources

BOOKS

Boles, John B. *The South through Time: A History of an American Region.* Englewood Cliffs, NJ: Prentice Hall, 1995.

Doherty, Kieran. *Soldiers, Cavaliers, and Planters: Settlers of the Southeastern Colonies.* Minneapolis: Oliver Press, 1999.

Dubowski, Cathy East. *Clara Barton: Healing the Wounds.* Englewood Cliffs, NJ: Silver Burdett Press, Inc., 1991.

Dubowski, Cathy East. *Robert E. Lee and the Rise of the South.* Englewood Cliffs, NJ: Silver Burdett Press, Inc., 1991.

Hakim, Joy. *Reconstruction and Reform.* New York: Oxford University Press, 1994.

Reger, James P. *Life in the South During the Civil War.* San Diego: Lucent Books, 1997.

WEB SITES

Explore St. Louis *www.st-louis-cvc.com*

Great Lakes Information Network *www.great-lakes.net*

The Great Lakes Shipwreck File 1679–1999
www.oakland.edu/boatnerd/swayze/shipwreck

Historic Deadwood *www.historicdeadwood.com*

LewisAndClarkTrail.com *www.lewisandclarktrail.com*

National Underground Railroad Freedom Center
www.undergroundrailroad.org

Ohio Public Library Information Network—Ohio History
www.oplin.lib.oh.us/index.cfm?ID=3-58

River Keepers *www.riverkeepers.org*

Index